RAPE OF REASON

The Corruption of the Polytechnic
of North London

KEITH JACKA

CAROLINE COX

JOHN MARKS

Published by CHURCHILL PRESS LIMITED
2 Cecil Court London Road Enfield Middlesex
Tel: 01-366 4551
1975

First published 1975 by Churchill Press Limited
© 1975

Printed in England by
Goron Pro-print Co. Ltd. Lancing Sussex BN15 8UF

Contents

Acknowledgements

We are grateful for the encouragement, advice and helpful comments we received from many people while we were planning and writing this book; in particular we would like to thank Christopher Champness. We thank also Diana Cookson and Christina Finch for their painstaking and accurate typing under great time pressures. Finally, we are deeply grateful for the unfailing support of our families throughout all the stresses involved both in writing the book and in living through the experiences it describes.

June 1975   K.J.

                                                                          C.C.

                                                                          J.M.

Prologue

The tower block—13 storeys of grey concrete looming above the roar of the giant lorries in Holloway Road; Ladbroke House, a converted factory at Highbury Barn in the heartland of the Arsenal Football Club; the squat red-brick ugliness of the Arts building in Kentish Town, opposite the Municipal Baths and Wash Houses; Camden Town, Essex Road, Marlborough House: dotted about several square miles of dense urban development, these are the buildings which house the educational and political activities of the Polytechnic of North London.

Inside are the classrooms, offices, lecture-halls, laboratories. In one room is a blackboard with a few words and hieroglyphics left written, visible scraps of a recent effort at accurate communication. Next door a small group of students and a teacher are discussing an essay, taking it apart and examining the ideas and phrases as a mechanic would investigate an intricate machine. The hour over, they drift out along the corridors.

TODAY !!! SMASH THE COURT OF GOVERNORS

In the clinical severity of the laboratory a sensitive needle-gauge registers the quantitative fact. Nearby a man repairs apparatus, surrounded by technical bric-a-brac—coloured wires, pliers, motors, coils, valves, meters—impedimenta for initiating the novice into an industrial civilisation.

```
┌─────────────────────────────────┐
│ ○ MILLERMAN HAS LOST CONTROL ○  │
│          OF HIS FACULTIES        │
│ ○                            ○  │
└─────────────────────────────────┘
```

The rows of books stretch out along the library shelves: the records of scholarship—history, economics, literature, mathematics—the bold statements, the subtle distinctions, the specialised language requiring years to master. There is quiet everywhere, and students reading: the sessions of silent thought.

But man cannot live by learning alone. Down in the canteen are the coffee cups, and release into the warm engulfing sea of noise. Soon the mass meeting begins: repetitive incantations, and the ruthless creed of unreason from the microphone. An end to judicious speech, and doubt. Oneness prevails. The flaring posters on the wall proclaim the Truth.

```
┌──────────────────────────┐
│ ○   THE FIGHT AGAINST  ○ │
│ ○ FASCISM BEGINS HERE ○  │
└──────────────────────────┘
```

1 The Seeds of Subversion

This book describes the sustained four-year siege of a college by those who would destroy or corrupt it, records the disruptive practices which have become established, analyses the conditions there which have made these possible, and considers the lessons of the situation for institutions of higher education and for liberal democratic societies.

The Polytechnic of North London (PNL) was created in February 1971 by merging the existing Northern Polytechnic (NP) and North Western Polytechnic (NWP). At its formation the college had about 4,000 full-time students, 3,000 part-time students, 550 academic staff and 550 non-academic staff, making it one of the largest of the polytechnics and bigger than many British universities.

Until the merger the two constituent colleges were unremarkable—no different from dozens of similar institutions throughout the country—but from the beginning the new college has been torn by internal strife and battered by continual disruption. It has provided regular copy for the national newspapers, and in educational circles has become a byword for trouble and disorder.

Disruption

Disruption kills the spirit of academic inquiry and can be lethal in an educational institution. It has been almost continuous since PNL was formed. The strategy of the Student Unions' (SU) Executive has never varied. Create an issue, agitate, then attack. Propaganda— hate-filled, sneering, vilifying to an astonishing degree —is the constant background to life at PNL. The difference at times of disruption is that a steady stream becomes a flood.

Here follows a chronological list of the main disruptions. It does not include the innumerable minor incidents—abusive speeches at meetings, attempts to stop meetings, etc.—such as would never occur in most academies.

1. Occupation of North Western Polytechnic: *23 February to 17 March 1971*

The most important, because it set the tone for all that followed—a tone of virulent hatred with a promise of relentless civil war. During the whole of that term there was a gigantic campaign against the Director-designate, Terence Miller. The endlessly repeated slogans were:

'Miller the racist'; 'Miller the authoritarian'; 'All power to the General Assembly of Staff and Students'.

2. Occupation of Northern Polytechnic: *28 February to 4 March 1971*

This was similar to the above, but a smaller affair.

3. Court of Governors: *Disruption of first meeting 1 March 1971*

This meeting was a style-setter, like the first occupation. In an important vote the two student Governors lost out. One of them, Terry Povey, left the room and returned with 50 students who stopped the meeting. Thus was inaugurated the tradition of meetings at PNL: if a critical vote goes against the SU executive, then student members break up the meeting.

4. Court of Governors: *26 April 1971*

This was held at County Hall under security guard, with militant students outside the meeting room. Mr Miller made his first formal appearance at a Polytechnic meeting as Director-designate by entering through a window; there was attempted disruption by sustained noise.

5. Academic Board: *15 December 1971 and 12 January 1972*
This, the inaugural meeting, was acrimonious, with very little business done. The reconvened meeting was abandoned after half an hour when the SU President refused to obey the Chairman's ruling to stop speaking.

6. Court of Governors: *March 1972*
This was disrupted by student Governor Mike Hill and the President of the National Union of Students (NUS), Digby Jacks. The ostensible reason was the freezing of SU funds.

7. Occupation (Camden, Ladbroke): *October 1972*
This occupation—on the 'Jenkins affair'—included a successful disruption by the SU executive of a press conference organised by PNL Conservative students.

8. Academic Board: *25 October 1972*
A group of students attended who were not members. They stayed and *voted* in favour of students being members of staff appointment panels.

9. & 10. Academic Board: *October/November 1972*
Two committees of the Academic Board were disrupted. Students who were not members attended and the meetings were abandoned.

11. Designation Ceremony: *28 November 1972*
The ceremony at the Queen Elizabeth Hall was wrecked. This was the SU executive's proudest exploit.

12. Academic Board: *29 November 1972*
Terry Povey refused to obey the Chairman's ruling; the meeting was abandoned with no business done.

13. Court of Governors: *14 May 1973*
This was a special meeting on the 'Jenkins affair'. The Director's motion—to remove Jenkins as Head of Department—seemed likely to pass. Student

Governor Terry Povey went out and brought in his troops, about 40 students. The meeting was abandoned and the motion was never resuscitated.

14. Court of Governors: *2 July 1973*
This was disrupted by student Governor Mike Hill, aided by a group of students outside with a steel band.

15. Occupation of administrative offices: *16 October 1973*
The Governors' meeting of 15 October 1973 did not pass a motion of no confidence in the Director, hence there was an occupation the next day. The *non*-academic staff forced the SU to call off this occupation by a threat of strike action. This was the first serious defeat of the SU executive.

After this stormy beginning the academic year 1973-4 was superficially quiet. A Joint Advisory Committee (Inner London Education Authority—ILEA—and PNL) had been set up to look into the affairs of what was by now a nationally notorious college; also, there was widespread student disgust with the SU executive, resulting in a series of General Meetings without a quorum. The executive spent their energies in propaganda, external activities (Oxford University, Essex University, City Polytechnic), and in lobbying the Joint Advisory Committee (JAC). Failing to get their way by lobbying, they recommended disruption in November 1974.

16. Academic Board: *7 November 1974*
Disruption was about to begin, but was foiled by a bomb scare, which cleared the building.

17. Court of Governors: *18 November 1974*
This was a notably savage disruption, a consequence of the previous Governors' meeting having passed a report which recommended a reduction (from 35 to 22 per cent) in student representation on the Academic Board.

18. Academic Board: *20 November 1974*

This was broken up after a few minutes, for the same reason.

Tactics

Disruption has clearly become a permanent feature of life at PNL. A common tactic is to advertise an SU meeting for the day *after* some important debate at the Court of Governors or the Academic Board. The climate of fear created by such pressures has influenced many decisions in the College. Some disruptions have been mandated by an SU meeting, others have been impromptu. Only the first occupation at NWP had large support and even there the support quickly dwindled. Typically the disrupters are a small minority. The SU executive has walked a tightrope between two situations: large numbers at an SU meeting means no direct action because the would-be disrupters are outnumbered; small numbers at the meeting may deny the activists a quorum.

There is a regular cycle in the warfare. It was accurately described to the authors by Mike Hill one day in a mood of careless boasting.[1] The cycle goes like this:

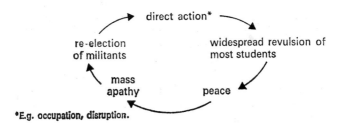

re-election of militants → direct action* → widespread revulsion of most students → peace → mass apathy → re-election of militants

*E.g. occupation, disruption.

---

[1] Mike Hill alternated with Terry Povey as SU President. Between them they ran the Unions of NWP, NP and then PNL, for about five years. Both are members of the International Socialists (IS).

The policy of disruption would probably have run out of steam long ago had not certain members of the academic staff given active support—by making inflammatory speeches at student meetings, passing motions in support of direct action by students, themselves participating in programmes of 'alternative education', and in other ways. The Association of Teachers in Technical Institutions (ATTI) has seldom opposed the student wreckers, and has even supported them.

Since the late 'sixties many colleges in Britain have been afflicted with disruption and occupations, but only the University of Essex has come near to PNL in the amount and the continuity of internal strife, and in no other college has there been such a breakdown in morale and college government.

The origin of PNL[1]

In 1966 the Department of Education and Science (DES) decreed that NP should merge with NWP to form a new polytechnic. The two colleges were quite different. NP had grown slowly; it was a stable, conservative institution run by a well-qualified, capable staff. It was noted for its excellence in the natural sciences and had a long tradition of vigorous research and post-graduate training in these fields. An Academic Board had been created but it was not important, nor was the SU; the departments were the real units of government in the college.

NWP was formed later than NP and was slow to find a coherent identity. From the mid-1950s it expanded rapidly, becoming in 10 years the largest polytechnic in inner London. The bias of the college, after many variations, moved towards the arts and the social sciences. Government was from the centre, the Principal having great power. In the late 1960s the

[1] C. Cox, B. Heraud, K. Jacka, J. Marks, R. Sullivan, *Notes on the Polytechnic of North London*, 1973 (copies available from the authors).

SU changed from a docile social club into a political force, self-confidently aggressive and willing to concern itself with any issue. Each year the executive became more politically radical and militant, and there was a parallel growth of radicalism amongst the staff. Working together, the student and staff radicals agitated in favour of strong student participation in college government. Opposition was half-hearted and the students ended by winning one-third of the places on the main Academic Board and even higher proportions on some Boards of Studies. This was by far the largest student representation of any comparable college in the country.

At its formation in 1971 the prospects for PNL looked superficially good, but the experienced observer could easily have foreseen trouble. For example, there were institutional weaknesses. Neither of the constituent colleges had been used to institutional autonomy. For validation of courses they leaned on the University of London, the Council for National Academic Awards (CNAA),[1] and various professional institutes. Their Academic Boards were recent creations and most members knew little of academic planning, nor had they experience of the stringent vetting of documents and the detailed supervision necessary to maintain academic standards. Also there were strong forces mobilised for assault from strategically powerful locations. Only a small fraction of academic staff was much worried by the extreme militancy of the NWP Students' Union or disturbed by the extraordinarily high degree of student representation (36 per cent) that had been agreed for the Academic Board of the newly-founded College. And even amongst this fraction probably no one guessed the loathsome nature of what was intended and later achieved by Mike Hill and his henchmen when, in a statement in December 1970 reported in the national press, he prophesied 'the most

[1] Established in the mid-1960s to validate degrees and to maintain academic standards in non-university colleges.

serious disturbances the country has yet seen at a polytechnic'.

Much of this book is an ugly history: of mass resentment and spite, of systematic attacks on institutional coherence, of sustained and often successful attempts to break down the integrity of individuals, of the ethical hollowness and failure of nerve of many in authority, and the ostrich mentality of others. In internal politics the record of most of the academic staff is deplorable.

But before continuing, we pause to describe another side to the life and work of PNL.

Academic achievements

It is only fair to document briefly the academic achievements of the College and to pay tribute to the good academic work being done by so many of our colleagues—both academic and non-academic staff—in circumstances more difficult, we suspect, than in any other institution of higher education in Britain. Such good work has been possible because of the nature of the academy—the fact that it is an unusually decentralised institution. This is a strength in that the periphery can function for a time even when the centre is almost paralysed, but a weakness in that the healthy peripheral sections tend to shrug off attacks on the centre as unimportant, apparently unaware that ultimately they cannot survive its demise.

Some afflicted departments will appear often in this book (for example, Sociology, Applied Social Studies), but despite the internal conflicts we portray, there are many staff and students in these departments who work conscientiously and maintain high academic standards. The best evidence for the high academic quality of most departments at PNL is the increase in the number of CNAA degree courses in the College. In November 1972, there were only nine CNAA degrees. Only two years later, 18 new degrees in a wide range of subjects had been submitted to the CNAA and approved. These new degree courses involved nearly all departments in the Polytechnic; most of them were undergraduate degrees (BA or BSc) but some were post-graduate courses (MSc). Anyone familiar with the mass of detailed, meticulous work required to submit even one degree to the CNAA will appreciate how much must have been done and the general high quality of the academic staff.

Blueprint for subversion

Two questions arise. How has it come about that an institution of higher education has degenerated to the level of violent disruption we have described? How long can those sectors of PNL which have built up a good and justified reputation maintain it in such an environment? We think that the primary cause of the degeneration at PNL has been the attempt to turn the Polytechnic into a revolutionary political base, and that PNL has no future as an academy unless this is realised and effectively countered.

The sequence of steps for converting an academy into a Red base has been spelt out in detail by Carl Davidson in 'Campaigning on the Campus'.[1] Since this sequence has been so meticulously followed at PNL by the student and staff activists we give here a brief summary:

1. Socialism on one campus is not feasible: 'We cannot liberate the university without radically changing the rest of society'.
2. The principal purpose of student power is to develop radical political consciousness amongst those who will later be in key positions in society. Aim at lower status and less well-established colleges rather than Ivy League universities. (In Britain: polytechnics, colleges of education, the Open University and the newer universities rather than Oxford or Cambridge.)

[1] Originally written for an American audience: included in *Student Power*, published jointly by Penguin and *New Left Review*, 1969.

3. Try to capture the internal media, including lecture series and meetings. Develop contacts with sympathisers in the external media. The aim is to de-sanctify or de-legitimise the authority of the institution.

4. Work from within existing student governments, but do not play by the rules. Student government 'can be used for . . . money . . . Money, without strings, is always a help. (At PNL the Student's' Union has a total income that is now around £68,000 per year.)

5. Demands should be for root and branch revolutionary changes, not reformist, piecemeal ones.

6. Don't organise 'Free Universities'—go for 'encroaching control': for example, SU to have control of 'the form and content of all political, social and cultural events'; students and staff, both individually and through their organisations, to control academic affairs.

7. Persuade teaching staff not to support the administration but in increasing order of preference: (*a*) remain neutral; (*b*) split; (*c*) support the radical activists.

8. 'Criticise (break up) classes in the classroom. Constantly criticise course structure, content, class sizes, the educational system and corporate capitalism.'

9. Disruption is the main source of power for radicals: 'Ultimately, we have access to only one source of power within the knowledge factory. And that power lies in our potential ability to stop the university from functioning . . . for limited periods of time'.

This is the strategic plan. Most of this book describes how the plan has been put into operation at PNL. But before we can fully understand how this has been done, we need an introductory analysis—about education, the nature of academies, and some prevalent world-views. This is given in Chapter 2.

*   *   *

First, however, we say a word about ourselves, which will partly explain why we wrote this book.

Keith Jacka—Childhood spent in the Australian bush; father a manual labourer and Communist Party member. The family moved to Melbourne, where he attended University (mathematics), but dropped out after two dissolute years.

For five years wandered about Australia as a labourer, interspersed with intervals in metropolitan bohemias. Short spell in the Communist Party ended after being expelled for refusing to tell expedient lies.

Completed a part-time degree in politics and history. Spent four years in scientific research (mathematics in medicine) in Melbourne and Harvard.

After two years in the South Sea Islands, came to England in 1962. Joined NWP in 1964 and teaches mathematics.

Politically inoculated early against totalitarianism. Brought up an atheist, but now sympathetic to religious belief.

Caroline Cox—Parents from top drawer; father a noted surgeon. Enjoyed a privileged Highgate childhood. Gained four A-levels but decided against university to become a nurse in Whitechapel (London Hospital).

Nursing career ended after contracting tuberculosis: on recovery stayed at home bringing up three children and studying part-time at Regent Street Polytechnic for a B.Sc. in Sociology (First Class, London University, 1967). Took M.Sc. (Econ.).

Head of the Sociology Department at PNL since March 1974; Open University tutor.

Nursing in the East End and the study of sociology changed her political attitudes from a reflex conservatism to left liberalism. Toughened by five years at PNL into an unrelenting opponent of everything totalitarian. A committed Christian: Anglican Franciscan.

John Marks—Son of intelligent working-class parents; father a lorry driver. At school a star pupil, conformist and good at games. Gained an open major scholarship to study physics at Cambridge where he was academically very successful, but experienced his first reservations about science.

After two years of National Service and short periods as a civil service scientist and school teacher, he completed a Ph.D. in physics at Middlesex Hospital.

Lectured for two years at a Swedish university before joining the staid Northern Polytechnic in 1966. Started as an innovator and still is, but has become a little wiser. Elected a member of the Court of Governors and of the Academic Board in 1968. Tutor for the Open University.

A member of the Labour Party and used to read *Observer, Guardian* and *New Statesman* with approval. In religion is a tolerant agnostic.

All three of us had doubts about the traditional educational structure, but as late as 1970 none of us had thought deeply about the themes of this book. For example, we had no strong feelings or clear ideas about student participation: we vaguely accepted it. Since then we have had to act in these matters, to study books about them, and to change our minds.

2 The Academy and its Alternatives

The world of a human being is informed by meanings; it is a world permeated by beliefs and understandings, especially about other persons and about himself. Like other creatures the humans go about the earth, observing birds, trees and the sky, but attending even more to the vast display of man-made meaningful things: buildings, mechanisms, printed words, pictures. Above all, they talk to one another, they exchange meanings. And because it is this way there is learning and education.[1]*

If human life were predetermined, a potential becoming manifest; if we were like plants and all were prefigured in the seed, the soil and the climate; in that case education would be an extra, a luxury. But life is not like that. Nobody is *born* human. To be human is to be historic rather than natural. A child reared apart from his own kind develops into a stunted thing, uncertain even how to walk.

What is education?

Education is a mediation, a transaction between the generations, where the new ones are inducted into that complex world of meanings which their elders inhabit. They are initiated into an inheritance of ideas: the gradations of good and bad, love and hate; the connections of justice and law; the precisions of

[1] M. Oakeshott, 'Education: the engagement and its frustration', in *Education and the Development of Reason,* edited by R. F. Dearden *et al,* Routledge and Kegan Paul, 1972.

*The sources on which we have drawn substantially are indicated by * in the Select Bibliography, pp. 147–148.

number, measurement, matter, motion. And none of these ideas can be handed over like objects; there is no giving of a key to a storehouse. They must be understood by the receiver, the learner, in a personal relation with one who knows.

Nor is education as simple as imitation, an imprinting by repetition of ready-made ideas and images. It is learning to look, listen, think, feel—above all to choose. But this will never occur unless the pupil is convinced of the value of learning, and this conviction will be enhanced or not according to his image of the teacher. The civilised inheritance of meanings must inspire pride, even reverence, in the teacher; he must be seen to cherish what he transmits, to gain strength and stature and fulfilment from it, else the interchange between the generations will be lifeless and ineffectual.

Contemporary debates about alternative views of education are dominated by two groups. Both believe that the interchanges in the classroom should be governed by extrinsic ends. One group believes that the nation needs first-class economists, doctors, mathematicians, etc. in order to be strong, wealthy, and make progress, and that we must hold to rigorous academic standards to produce these virtuosos. The other group believes that the drive for social equality should predominate over all else, and would use schools and universities as the main instruments for achieving equality, however much they are changed in the process. But education as we have described it has to be an end in itself irrespective of the external purposes it may also serve. And this applies at all levels —from elementary school to the post-graduate classes at universities.

This brings us to a matter of nomenclature. Typically we shall use the word 'academy' to refer to any institution of higher education whose purposes include those which we have commended. In Britain, for example, as well as the universities, the polytechnics come within this field. To justify this inclusion, and for other reasons, we turn now to the development of higher education.

The university

In spite of the changes in the form and content of people's lives over the last 700 years the university in the Western world remains recognisably the same institution as it was in the 13th century, in the days of prestige of the University of Paris. The model was the medieval craft-guild, and as in the guild there were three grades of membership: student (apprentice), Bachelor of Arts (journeyman), and Master of Arts (master). Members of the university subscribed to the four fundamental guild assumptions: that all belonged to the same organisation and owed loyalty to it; that there are stages in learning, but no impenetrable barriers; that learners half-way through the stages may help to teach beginners; that learning is a craft, and since masters have a monopoly they are responsible for defending standards.

The stages of membership and the four basic guild assumptions can still be discerned in the structure and operation of contemporary academies the world over. Naturally, these are the features which infuriate the extreme progressive critics of our time. Since the medieval institutions of monastery and craft-guild were abolished centuries ago they think that one big push will likewise sweep the archaic, élitist, medieval university into 'the dustbin of history'. We oppose these progressive critics, not because we idolise tradition but because we consider the original form of the university to be essentially sound, well suited to its purposes both then and now.

Its idea and purpose

We start with a précis of the views of three men of our time on what is the informing principle, the 'Idea', of a university. They all accept the university as a valuable institution. They know its history from medieval times until the present day; and they know, too, its short-comings, but they do not wish to change it radically—rather to strengthen it by removing parasitic growths, and by reaffirming its central purpose.

First is Karl Jaspers, Professor of Philosophy at Heidelberg until suspended by the Nazis in 1937:

> 'The university is a community of scholars and students engaged in the task of seeking truth. It derives its autonomy from the idea of academic freedom, a privilege granted to it by state and society which entails the obligation to teach truth in defiance of all internal or external attempts to curtail it. Ideally the student thinks independently, listens critically, and is responsible to himself.'[1]

Next, Robert Nisbet, a contemporary American sociologist:

> 'The university is built on the dogma: Knowledge is important· (Not "relevant" knowledge; not "practical" knowledge; simply knowledge.) There are two equally venerable traditions: prophetic knowledge, and scholarship. The first tradition (Plato, Descartes) asserts that true knowledge is available to the man of pure reason irrespective of his knowledge of texts. The second (university) tradition values also reason, intuition, commonsense, but it emphasises monumentally the idea of cumulative corporate knowledge; texts are indispensable. All modern disciplines, including the sciences, arose first in the West on the basis of a study of texts and commentaries within the universities.'

> 'The university was always imbued with the idea of service to society. But such service was indirect, by providing, for example, a unique environment for young minds through their disciplined exposure to scholarship.'[2]

Finally, Kenneth Minogue, a British political theorist:

> 'Academic inquiry is not the same thing as rationality or intellectuality. Because a modern university educates people who later become administrators and technologists it does not follow that the essence of a university lies in its training of such persons. Education—the inculcation of standards of excellence—often misfits a person for the life he will lead . . . The academic world is indifferent to opinion; it is concerned

[1] K. Jaspers, *The Idea of the University*, Peter Owen, 1960.

[2] R. Nisbet, *The Degradation of the Academic Dogma*, Heinemann, 1971.

only with knowledge. With the academic everything is up for discussion; there is no permanence in truth. He is concerned with the quest, not the goal.'[1]

These three men emphasise different aspects of what they agree is the central purpose of a university.

To preserve, transmit and extend knowledge. As described above, this is the classical tradition. We shall argue throughout this book that, whatever other purposes are possible within an academy and can be accommodated there, if they seriously conflict with this traditional aim then the academy is likely to have its identity weakened and thence to fall apart or to be transformed beyond recognition. An academy which manifests this central purpose is usually described as an 'ivory tower' by those who would destroy it, who regard it as incorrigibly 'élitist', 'a bastion of privilege', an institution of 'the ruling class'.

Various other purposes are commended as appropriate for an academy. We shall discuss the more significant ones, indicating whether they are compatible with the central purpose.

To train students in the advanced skills of the society. This function of an academy has a history as ancient and respectable as the first. The medieval law school of Bologna University was even more famous in its day than the Massachusetts Institute of Technology in ours, and for similar reasons. In practice there is often a tension between the functions of knowledge and training, although this may well be a creative tension, particularly at higher levels of knowledge and skill. It was this tension which led the Germans in the 19th century to create institutions of higher technology, the Technische Hochschulen, quite separate from the existing universities.

[1] K. R. Minogue, *The Concept of a University*, Weidenfeld & Nicolson, 1973.

Community resource: the service-station academy.[1] In this view the academy's central function should be *directly* to solve the problems of the society of which it is a part; problems, for example, in agriculture, manufacture, commerce, government, war, social welfare, race relations, environmental improvement. A common method is to set up self-contained institutes or study-groups on the campus, often funded and controlled from outside, or to put together *ad hoc* training courses for the personnel required to handle the problem. This invasion of the academy is less common in Britain than in the USA where, at the height of the Cold War, much of the finance and activities in science and technology in many of the academies was directly controlled by the military. But it would have been equally inimical to the academies if the activities had been humanitarian rather than warlike—crash programmes of poverty control and racial integration, for example.

Here is a statement from an author who advocates the transformation of the academy into a community resource:

'. . . the essential feature of the polytechnic as an urban community university, as a people's university, must be its responsibility and responsiveness to the democracy rather than its insulation from it.'[2]

If what the masses consider most important at the time is to be the main criterion for allocating resources, then the researcher with unconventional views (often just the person whose work turns out to be most seminal) will soon be starved of funds; public opinion is seldom sympathetic to unorthodoxy.

The community resource purpose, if it becomes dominant, destroys the integrity of the academy in several ways. Firstly, it reduces the autonomy of the academy and makes impossible any strong commitment to the steady pursuit and transmission of knowledge.

[1] R. Nisbet, *op. cit.*; J. Searle, *The Campus War*, Pelican, 1972.

[2] E. Robinson, *The New Polytechnics*, Penguin, 1969.

Resources are not assessed and assigned according to the deliberations of a group of academic peers, but depend on the variable policies of governments and outside pressure-groups, who have often no interest in the long-term flourishing of the academy.

Secondly, the quality of education will usually deteriorate. In an academic department where some of the staff are engaged in *direct* social improvement as part of their work, there will be a pressure on the students, and many will come to see academic studies as trivial and remote, irrelevant to the 'vital problems of the age'; even worse, they may fall a lifelong prey to the sterilities of an ideology.

Thirdly, it poisons relations amongst the scholarly experts by creating inequalities. It is essential for the health of the academy that the Shakespearian scholar has equal pay and status, and sits on the same committees, as the expert in space medicine, or astrophysics.

We are advocating the autonomy of the academy and its insulation from society, but we support the idea of the academy's serving society. It has always done so, and never more than in the early days of the medieval university. But the academy serves society best by doing so indirectly. We are not arguing that huge sums of money should be poured into academies and locked up there—rather the reverse. The structure of the academy is appropriate for certain tasks— teaching, scholarship, some kinds of research—but it is not obvious that it is the best institution for carrying out large-scale industrial or scientific research, and it is clear that it is institutionally incompetent to lead towards a better life those who are deprived, such as certain ethnic minorities, and the poor.

Youth city: the academy as a city-state of the young.[1] Nowadays many students have an idea of the academy, seldom articulated but easily abstracted from a quick

---

[1] J. Searle, *op. cit.*

glance at almost any student newspaper. It is what you would expect from an affluent Western society: a misplaced consumer's view—hedonistic, permissive, and parasitic. From the department store they take the notion that the student (the customer) is always right and should be offered a continually varying smorgasbord of delights. From the media they learn that the academy should be exciting, entertaining, relevant to their personal needs, and that they can switch programmes or turn them off at will.

In short, they believe that the purpose of an academy is to satisfy the needs and desires of the young, from the provision of round-the-clock therapy to serving as a base in a campaign for the spread of Consciousness III, and that the academic and non-academic staff are there only to minister to them. Naturally these students see no sense in examinations and grades—some are outraged at their very existence, and cannot understand how anyone could expect them to submit to such intolerably archaic repression. They take for granted that the academy should be organised as an open democracy—one man, one vote for all members; and, if you agree with their estimate of purpose, they are quite right.

It is no use asking where the money is coming from, why the older members of a society should trouble to subsidise endlessly and unconditionally such a parasitic community. You will never be answered if you ask such a question. Those who see the academy as a youth city have never encountered such questions at any time in their lives. They have grown up with the uncontested assumption that three years in an academy at the beginning of their adult life is not something to be grateful for—it is their inalienable right. And only a puzzled resentment will ensue if the question is pressed.

We believe that this doctrine, of the academy as an egalitarian youth city, is very pervasive, that it is significant to varying degrees in the minds of most

students in the Western world. Typically it is under-
ground, never brought out into daylight and critically
examined; and its subterranean magnetic influence
warps all discussion on academic government, especially on the issue of student representation.

*Dissent: the academy as conscience of society and
guardian of dissent.* Some would prefer that the
academy should concentrate on fostering the good and
subverting the bad, that it should be the institution
which supports those who disagree with the received
opinions in society.

This is an error of emphasis, perhaps deriving from
confusion about the nature of academic freedom. Of
course, the academy should support dissent, but only
partially and indirectly: by the staff pursuing ideas
wherever they may lead, and by the training of students
to examine critically whatever is presented so that
later, outside the academy, they will have some
notion of what it means to examine a doctrine with
detachment. But a parliamentary faction, or a group of
competent journalists—these are far better and more
legitimately placed as professional dissentients than
the academy can or should ever be. Commitment to a
perpetually critical attitude to what counts as knowledge is not at all the same as a commitment to dissent,
and presuppositions which lead one to favour doctrines
simply because they go counter can be quite as
stifling as their opposites. From the academic viewpoint there is no particular merit in being either orthodox
or unorthodox.

Political base: the academy as a base for revolution.

'The emergent student revolutionaries aim to turn the tables on
the system, by using its universities and colleges as base areas
from which to undermine key institutions of the social order.
No advanced capitalist state can afford to maintain a permanent police occupation of all colleges and universities, nor
can it act like a Latin-American military thug and simply
close down the universities which after all are necessary, in

the long run, to the productive process. So long as the universities and colleges provide some sort of space which cannot be permanently policed they can become "red bases" of revolutionary agitation and preparation.'[1]

This is refreshingly explicit and describes what has happened to some of the universities on the Continent, particularly in West Germany, over the last decade. Nor is this surprising. For the academy, because of its essentially liberal nature, cannot easily protect itself against alien forces. It depends for its integrity on the *esprit de corps* of its members. But this purpose—the academy as a political base—is an interim one. After the revolution, what then? Unfortunately we are given no coherent answer, only vague mystifications expressed in the stupefyingly scholastic jargon of neo-Marxism.

This covers most of the objectives typically proposed for academies. We have indicated, explicitly or implicitly, those that we consider should be directly aimed at, those that should be achieved indirectly, and those that we consider destructive. The essential purposes of the academy were embodied in the organisation of the medieval universities. These purposes still hold, but life has changed since AD 1200. There has been an expansion of knowledge, both in depth and breadth, and many shifts of emphasis. This has produced great changes in academic curricula and also new kinds of institutions of higher education, notably the technological academies. We turn now to these matters.

Science and technology in British academies[2]

Science did not gain a foothold in British universities until the foundation of the University of London in 1826. But little further happened until the 1850s. From then on the intellectual battle for the accommodation of science was fought, especially in Oxford and

[1] R. Blackburn and A. Cockburn (eds.), *Student Power*, Penguin, 1969, p. 17.

[2] E. Ashby, *Technology and the Academics*, Macmillan, 1966.

Cambridge, by drawing on the German tradition of Wissenschaft—the empirical, hypothetical attitude to *all* knowledge, including physical science. In this tradition the vocation of science is just as honourable a calling as that of the historian or classical scholar.

This rise of the science faculties in the European universities from the early 19th century onwards led to the dominant modern academic attitude to knowledge and truth. It is not essentially different from the medieval attitude, but has differences of emphasis. Knowledge is now seen as an open system. Truth is not something final and sacrosanct. It is held firmly yet tentatively and is constantly being modified, enlarged and adjusted. The doctrine has generated an institutional code for tolerating error. If truth is tentative, then error becomes simply an alternative interpretation. Both accepted truth and presumed error can be challenged and must submit themselves to examination. But there is a discipline of dissent, including a consensus of opinion about the criteria for knowledge. Discovery is rigorously tested and then accepted on its merits, irrespective of the status and social origins of the discoverer. This is a very subtle doctrine indeed, a remarkable creation, well understood and faithfully practised in their laboratories by most scientists, although seldom articulated.

Technology was accepted into the British universities in the late 19th century because of the need for manager-technologists in industry who could hold their own with their counterparts from the Continent of Europe. Unlike pure science, it was tolerated rather than assimilated. It was not difficult for the universities to adapt to scientific thought (the metaphysician and the theoretical physicist are not so far removed), but the technologist is an awkward newcomer. The master of an expertise of profound significance, he straddles the realms of theory and practice and so far no one has found the laws and ceremonies to civilise without emasculating him.

Academic drift

Time and again over the past hundred years a college
founded in the technical college tradition has gradually
transformed itself into a university.[1] This process has
been documented by J. Pratt and T. Burgess[2] under
the name of 'academic drift'. It persisted until the
mid-1960s when, soon after the conversion of
10 CATS[3] into universities, the reigning Labour
Government tried to stem the tide. There would, they
said, be no more new universities in the foreseeable
future; instead, the policy would be to foster the
polytechnics as separate institutions of higher education[4] within what was called the 'Binary System'.

Pratt and Burgess suggest that this was an attempt
not merely to halt but even to reverse the process of
academic drift. However, they consider that the
attempt is failing:

'The polytechnics have already embarked on the process of
aspiration and many will be recognisably institutions in the
university tradition.'[5]

Furthermore, they say:

'The elevation of the polytechnics to university status will
no doubt take place amidst great public acclaim. But the loss
to the public sector will be irreparable, and the loss of opportunity to the traditional students unforgiveable.'[6]

There seems to be some confusion. First, Pratt and
Burgess merge aspiration to *formal* university status
with aspiration to higher levels of academic work. We
are indifferent to the former but support the latter; we
believe that polytechnics should become 'academies',

[1] The Manchester area has some notable examples: Owens College, founded in the
1850s, eventually became the University of Manchester; the Municipal School
of Technology (founded 1902) acquired university status in 1956 as the
Institute of Science and Technology; the present University of Salford grew
from roots in the old Salford Technical College. Most recently, the John Dalton
College of Technology was incorporated into Manchester Polytechnic.

[2] J. Pratt and T. Burgess, *Polytechnics: A Report,* The Pitman Press, Bath, 1970.

[3] Colleges of Advanced Technology.

[4] White Paper, *A Plan for Polytechnics and Other Colleges,* Cmnd. 3006, 1966.

[5] J. Pratt and T. Burgess, *op. cit.,* p. 54.

[6] J. Pratt and T. Burgess, *op. cit.* p. 177.

in the sense outlined earlier. Secondly, they imply that polytechnics will abandon those students whom traditionally they should be serving. But why should this be so? By tradition polytechnics are more flexible than universities. They provide a wide range of courses for a very heterogeneous body of students: full and part-time courses during both day and evening, sandwich courses, short intensive courses, etc. And the qualifications are equally varied: degrees, diplomas, professional certificates. Continuing this tradition will enable the polytechnics to fulfil their distinctive function, which is to make genuine *higher* education available to a greater diversity of people. There is no necessary negative association between this valuable function and the phenomenon of academic drift. Therefore, like Pratt and Burgess we observe the phenomenon, but unlike them we welcome it.

Academic imperatives

Why have so many colleges experienced this 'drift'? Pratt and Burgess explain it mainly in terms of status and money; but this explanation seems inadequate, for the shifts are also intellectual and educational.

The early technical colleges were founded as institutions of strictly useful knowledge, but in time most of them have shifted to a middle ground, laying equal emphasis on the pursuit of knowledge for its own sake; and if this shift does not occur the college will remain for ever parasitic on the genuine academies. The poverty of imagination and impersonality of a purely utilitarian curriculum soon become unbearably oppressive to all but the most prosaic of temperaments amongst staff and students. Not only this, it is also intellectually enfeebling and can even be ineffective. For the solution of a difficult practical problem often derives from the results of pure research on fundamentals, even though such research had no obvious practical application at the time. The evolution we discuss is not unique to Britain: there have been similar developments in such world-famous academies as the Ecole Polytechnique in France, the Massachusetts Institute of Technology in the USA, and the Technische Hochschulen in Germany.

If certain *academic* imperatives are the main cause of academic drift, then to oppose them in the polytechnics will be to stunt their natural academic development and impair their educational effectiveness. But some persons do advocate just this—in the name of 'comprehensive higher education'.

Comprehensive higher education

The term is often used, but loosely, and covers a wide spread of meanings. The White Paper on Polytechnics[1] refers to something close to what we have commended—an institution of higher education with a diversity of courses and students—but many writers talk of a 'people's university':

> 'It could offer a comprehensive range of courses, from honours degrees to part-time work with little academic content. Instead of an institution in which monastic autonomy is seen as a guarantee of academic objectivity the comprehensive university would be open to all the pressures of society—from students, staff, politicians, even industry.'[2]

We have already indicated how some of these ideas are antithetical to the nature of an academy. Besides this, the statement ignores certain difficult problems. How would such a hybrid institution be governed? How would its 'academic' section maintain standards? And how large would such a college need to be? There are growing pressures on the polytechnics to move towards this kind of 'comprehensivisation',[3] and as yet there is little effective opposition. Few people in academies (either universities or polytechnics) are explicitly committed to a coherent philosophy of

---

[1] Cmnd. 3006, 1966, *op. cit.*

[2] Peter Scott in *The Times Higher Education Supplement (THES)*, 28 April 1973.

[3] For example, in *THES*, 25 April 1975.

higher education and hence have no firm anchorage for resisting the pull of alternatives. Others openly advocate antithetical models. For example, a current polytechnic director writes:

'The principle that the Local Authority has the right to control and conduct the curriculum of the polytechnic or college is, I think, quite indisputable. The institution is there to serve the community and not to serve the particular interests of the staff who happen to be working there. This is the basic difference and the sooner we recognise it the better. If decisions are unpalatable, as they often are, there is but one consolation: in a democracy one has on many occasions to "democ", i.e. to accept the decision of elected representatives. If one is not prepared to do this one is led to the situation where a little man with a moustache and a swastika will be telling us what to do.'[1]

It may be valuable to retain the present differences of emphasis between universities and polytechnics, but the two sectors cannot be underwritten by fundamentally different principles. Higher education is not divisible, since the central purpose is always the same: to preserve, extend and transmit knowledge. But some recent developments in polytechnics run counter to this purpose and the universities would be wise to watch these developments closely; otherwise they may awake one morning in the City of Academia to find a Trojan Horse within the gates.

The academy as an institution

For any institution to function successfully its structure and government must be closely matched to its purposes. This is especially true of an academy since, as we have seen, its main purposes are more compli-cated than those of most institutions and it is not easy to estimate the quality of its work. An academy is necessarily a very decentralised institution since it can only operate effectively if its individual academic staff possess *academic authority* and can work in conditions

[1] G. Brosan (North East London Polytechnic), in the *Technical Journal,* February 1974.

which guarantee their *academic freedom*. These two concepts must be discussed before the characteristic and unusual features of academic government can be understood.

Academic freedom[1]

Generally, when we use the word 'freedom' we shall refer to situations where there is a choice among realistic alternatives, a chance to change one's mind, room to manoeuvre. A man is not free to travel if he is living from hand to mouth and the only mode of travel is by privately-owned motor car. Also: to speak without ambiguity of freedom, or of being free, we must specify *who* is free, what he is free *from*, and what he is free to *do*.

The classical theory of academic freedom can be summarised as: the staff member is free to teach and to research, within the constraints of academic criteria, according to his judgement and unimpeded by government, external public opinion, or by the threat of disruption if he violates the canons of some internal self-appointed group of censors. The student is free to study and learn, guided by the teachers but with a view to reaching his own conclusions. Like the staff member he also is guaranteed freedom from pressures and threats, both external and internal. This is a theory of one kind of institution and how it best works. It does not tell us how to run a hospital, or a factory, or a broadcasting studio, nor is it a theory of society.

The theory is based on four claims:
1. *Knowledge is valuable*. This is an axiom; it can hardly be proved by experiment.
2. *An academy is an institution for advancing and transmitting knowledge*. This is a definition.
3. *The best way to gain and test knowledge is by free inquiry*, rather than, for example, by a reverential

[1] J. Searle, *op. cit*.

submission to the literal truth of ancient texts, or to the dictates of a government or a bullying pressure-group. This claim is part of a theory of knowledge.

4. *The academic staff, because of their special knowledge, are fitted to teach and research in ways that other members of the academy are not.* This is a denial of full internal democracy. The academy is an aristocracy of a certain kind of trained intellect.

Academic authority[1]

The notion of academic standards assumes that there is a field of knowledge associated with each academic discipline, and that it takes ability, time and effort to understand it. An individual achieving such understanding gains *natural* academic authority, which is what is being estimated in making staff appointments. The criteria are: qualifications, subject knowledge, experience, logical coherence in discussion, and ability to teach. On appointment, a staff member is vested with *formal* academic authority by the institution.

The authority of the teacher in the classroom derives originally from his being an office-holder (lecturer, professor, etc). Typically, he gains *personal* authority as time passes—strengthening it by care and competence in the classroom and amongst his peers, or weakening it by displaying inadequate knowledge, or by indifference to the needs of his students. Although the foundation of his authority is his subject expertise, it is also necessary that he be continuously active in sharing his knowledge, and that the students wish to learn. His authority is circumscribed by: his field of expertise and the responsibilities vested in him by the institution; the rules of logic and evidence, binding on all; the existence of individual judgement, which is a corrective to any over-emphasis of the principle of

[1] E. Ashby and M. Anderson, *The Rise of the Student Estate in Britain,* Macmillan 1969.

authority. But in seeking truth in an academic context, individual judgement is only a starting point for a revision of public judgement.

Authority in the classroom is fundamental, but it is fragile, depending on courteous behaviour from all. Nor can it be backed up by coercion; its only safeguard is the *esprit de corps* of the main body of staff and students, and their commitment to the central aims of the academy. Only a minute span of learning and experience is effectively open to private verification, so that if a student loses faith in the integrity of all authority, if he decides he can have no trust in the competence and honesty of his teachers, then he will be labouring under great burdens and his education will be hindered accordingly.

Opponents of academic authority unfailingly refuse to discriminate between authority—an essential principle in any community or institution—and its pathological manifestation, authoritarianism, which is the *abuse* of one's position of authority, especially by taking decisions without reasonable consultation.

Joining and leaving an academy

An academy is a voluntary association; there are entry qualifications, but members may leave it at will. The obvious contrast is the nation-state. A young person qualifies automatically for full citizenship at 18 years, is given unasked an array of rights, and bears the burden of a set of obligations. A voluntary association has an advantage over a compulsory one: it can select its members, making entry as rigorous as it pleases. And this holds quite strictly for academic staff who, before being accepted, must pass stringent tests which are essentially the same as those devised 750 years ago in the Middle Ages. The parallel goes further. Just as in medieval times there was a network of academies, national and international, a multiplicity of institutions, all roughly the same size and doing the same kind of work, so it is today. And there is much coming and going between them: interchange of staff, conferences of experts, communications in learned journals. This is the way in which the standing of an academy, and of the scholars within it, is assessed.

Until the 20th century the situation for students was also much as it had always been. The academy was a voluntary association, with specified entry requirements—selecting only those who seemed intellectually and temperamentally suitable—and rigorous in its accreditation tests. But the rise of the doctrine of 'Higher Education for All' has changed that. If in a modern industrialised nation the qualification for most good jobs is to have studied at an academy for at least three years, then it is less true to say that *for the student* the academy is a voluntary association, that he is free not to join. This change alone is enough to explain much of the violence on the campuses of the Western world since the early 'sixties.

Academic government[1]

For an institution to endure the members must often act as one. This proceeds from agreement, a difficult objective often requiring patient persuasion and prolonged argument. Politics is the activity of striving for this agreement, which then leads to decisions, policies, and their execution, the province of government. In this sense every academy has a government and is an arena for internal politics. But the *political models* appropriate to this internal politics must be compatible with the concepts of academic freedom and academic authority. Political analogies with institutions of government in the wider society seldom apply in an academy, and if they are pressed can often undermine its central purposes. We will now discuss some political models, including both those we think

[1] G. C. Moodie and R. Eustace, *Power and Authority in British Universities*, Allen & Unwin, 1974.

appropriate to an academy and those which are inimical to it.

Consensual democracy exists in an organisation when decisions are reached after discussion amongst equals leading to a consensus without the fiat of a superior authority. In an academy ruled in this way the citizenry—those who have to be consulted—are usually taken to be primarily the members of the academic staff. Citizenship derives from academic expertise.

The most significant recurrent decisions in an academy concern what is taught (curriculum), who is taught (admissions), how they are tested (assessments), who teaches (appointments), and where knowledge is extended (research). On these matters there is nothing even approaching a chain of command. Decision-making is very decentralised, all academic staff taking part to some extent, and a consensus is both the ideal and often close to what does happen; modified, however, by the recognition of areas of competence, which leads to a natural division of labour and a departure from pure equality.

It is an ideal much favoured by academics, but consensual democracy has serious drawbacks. It is very slow, since decisions are usually made by tactful and informal consultation between all interested parties; hence it is least useful when you most need it—in a time of crisis. It is effective for internal departmental matters, but not much use for disputes between departments, or for the relations of the academy with the external society. Also, it depends upon uniformity of values. A small intransigent nucleus can easily stymie the procedure. Consensual democracy appeals because it appears to avoid overt conflict; it seems a sympathetic urbane procedure of rational discussion leading to wise and just decisions. But even this very restrictive form of democracy (academic staff only) cannot perform all of the tasks of decision within an academy; it has to be supplemented with other procedures.

Oligarchy is rule by the few. Typically the word is pejorative, meaning rule by a few who have secretly or unjustly gained power and use it despotically. But in its neutral sense the word obviously does describe aspects of academic government. The Vice-Chancellor or Director and his Deputy, the active Heads of Department and a few others who sit on some key committees—in total, say, a score of persons—have a large amount of power and influence in the governing of an academy. But this power is quite circumscribed because their initiatives must be acceptable to some larger body such as a Senate or Academic Board. An even deeper reason for the limited power of an academic oligarch derives from the fundamental activities of an academy, as already described. To give of his best in the classroom or laboratory the lecturer or researcher needs a clear run. There his autonomy is almost complete.

Representation. Academies are distinctive in two ways: their problems lie towards the expert end of the scale, and professional autonomy is seen as a necessity for the highest levels of academic work. These are the justifications for special governmental rights being given to the academic staff.

However, there are other interest groups in the academy, notably the numerically largest body, the students, but also the non-academic staff. Also there are limits to the relevance of expert authority: in some areas of institutional organisation there is no natural unchallengeable authority. Hence the demand by groups other than academic staff for representation on governmental bodies of the academy.

Nowadays the principle of representation of relevant members is widely used in constituting academic committees. Students, for example, are strongly represented on committees governing halls of residence, and on bodies concerned with student discipline. They usually have an autonomous student union and run their own newspaper. These developments have occurred peacefully, but the battle-lines have been drawn around the issue of participation (rather than consultation) in academic decision-making.

Two limitations are typical in universities that have student participation:

1. The number of students on committees is restricted, usually to 50 per cent or less on welfare committees and to a much smaller percentage on academic ones.

2. Certain areas, such as appointments, promotions and examinations, are classified as reserved; students are not to be present at discussions.

This line has been generally held in British *universities*,[1] but not in the *polytechnics*. The percentages of students on polytechnic academic boards are often quite high, and there are usually no reserved areas.[2]

Participatory democracy[3]

An alternative principle is widely advocated. It goes by the name of participatory democracy. The theory is so simple it can be described in a few lines.[4] The basic academic unit would consist of, say, about a thousand people—a 'school'. The academy as a whole would be a loose federation of several schools. Day-to-day running of the school would be done by a small committee of around 20 people, containing representatives of all main groups, but ultimate power would lie with a General Assembly of the people, i.e. everyone in the school: teachers, researchers, undergraduates,

[1] D. A. Bell *et al*, 'A Survey of Student Representation on University Senates', *Universities Quarterly*, Winter 1972.

[2] C. Cox and J. Marks, 'Student Representation in Polytechnics', *Universities Quarterly*, Spring 1975.

[3] D. Martin, 'The Ugly Face of Participatory Democracy', *THES*, 5 April 1974.

[4] D. Rubinstein and C. Stoneman, *Education for Democracy*, Penguin, 1970, p. 203.

post-graduates, technical staff, secretarial staff, maintenance and service staff. The General Assembly would be the sovereign body, would meet fairly frequently, and would have the right of veto and instant recall of representatives. In the general assembly all would have equal voting rights.

It is not so much a theory of *academic* government as a theory of government for all institutions, as is often admitted by its supporters. It is in fact essentially the theory of the Workers' Councils, the Soviets, which have arisen briefly during times of revolutionary fervour in Europe in the last hundred years.

Taking participatory democracy as a serious proposal suggests the following questions. How often do you need to consult the will of the general assembly: once a day, once a month? And would not this make for wild zig-zags of decisions? Also, are there no rights of sub-groups, no guarantees for individuals, no areas of autonomy for those who do not wish to be entirely governed by the general will? A little thought or a minimum of experience of participatory democracy will show why in practice it quickly degenerates into a singularly unpleasant form of government with strong leanings to totalitarianism. The reason is that everything becomes political; there are no walls behind which to retreat and quietly work or think. You must forever watch and suspect your neighbour.

The ones who rise are the rabble-rousers, those with quick manipulative minds, glib-tongued and unrestrained by scruples. The able but thoughtful, and those with independent minds who cannot please the crowd, stand no chance against the politicos. All that an academy stands for and all of the immense value of an intelligent division of labour, is thrown away. Participatory democracy is likely to lead to an extreme form of precisely that which it is ostensibly opposed to: an apathetic mass manipulated by an inner group which uses all the familiar modern techniques of media domination to produce a spurious unanimity. Typically this inner group manifests an extreme hypocrisy and operates a system of authority far more arbitrary and intolerant of criticism than anything which preceded it.

We have claimed that the government of an academy depends on the fundamental principle that authority derives from a specific kind of knowledge. Clearly participatory democracy denies this. Assuming, then, that the students and staff who profess the doctrine have not abandoned rationality, they must hold to some view of the world and the academy radically different from the one we have presented. We shall single out what seem to us the three most important components of this different view: spontaneity, extreme relativism and ideology. For many participatory democrats all three elements are present, but the proportions vary greatly.

The dogma of spontaneity[1]

A (self-styled) spontaneous person denies all but the purely human. He believes that everyone is born free, with unlimited potency for experience— but unlike the others he fights to retain this potency. He rejects all distinctions based on age, class, division of labour. There is only one meaningful distinction: between the truly real, authentic genuine people—who know that a repressive society is for ever attempting to alienate them from pure being—and the squares, the conventionals, who have given in, sold their birthright for a procrustean set of rights and duties, and the status and affluence that go with it. A real person exists in two modes only: as one, utterly unique and private; or submerged in the all, the oceanic infinity. He is one and unique when . . . like man, it comes to him straight . . . he just knows, recognises; he is submerged when it is all happening—the music, the lights, everyone far out on acid or whatever.

[1] D. Martin, 'Order and Rule', in *Tracts Against the Times*, Lutterworth Press, 1973.

Real people cannot be classified or graded in any hierarchy of skill or knowledge, because true knowledge is incommunicably personal. So there is no such thing as differences of knowledge between persons; that is all a con of the squares, the non-authentic ones. Likewise there is no personal cumulation of knowledge, because all that is truly real is immediate, situated and alive. Learning is seen as an expansion of consciousness and the only legitimate function of education is to provide an arena for personal development. Teachers are redundant because one is not taught *by* somebody, one grows into knowledge. Science is particularly offensive as the paradigm of dry rational cumulation. Science affirms rules which can be understood only by accepting the hard otherness of the external world. It sets forth an order and stability in which personality is irrelevant.

Extreme relativism[1]

Consider this statement: 'There is no one truth in which the university can educate us. We have to find our own version of the truth for ourselves and what may be true for one person may well be untrue for another.'[2] And this: 'By contrast we are using the term "knowledge" to refer . . to *all* thought forms which are used by individuals in a society as a basis of everyday life.'[3] Each of these statements has the flavour of relativism. If he is emphasising the individual vision the relativist maintains that all judgement can be reduced to personal taste or belief. Knowledge is therefore only opinion dressed in fine clothes. If the group is being emphasised the relativist will reduce judgement to the sub-culture, the social setting, the historical background.

[1] S. Wilson, 'Truth', Unit 10 of *Problems of Philosophy*, A303, Open University Press, 1973.

[2] S. Scoffham, student at the University of Kent, *Guardian*, 9 May 1972.

[3] The Open University, *The Construction of Reality*, E 282, section 3.32, 1971.

We have not the space here to analyse the different kinds of relativism, but this does not matter because we are mainly concerned with certain absurdly exaggerated versions of the doctrine and the attacks on the academy derived from them. The insight of the relativist is not new. For the last few centuries the novelists have been recording for us with marvellous skill the world as seen from a variety of viewpoints. But nonetheless the novelists, as much as the scientists, have always implicitly assumed that there is *one* universe, greater and all-inclusive of the worlds they are temporarily portraying; and that somehow all of the partial views can be reconciled.

Unfortunately, intellectual relativism is not even the beginning of a solution to the problems of knowledge; it is an avoidance of them by denying their existence. There is in it a gigantic error right from the start. Take the statement above by the student. Presuming that he wants it to be meaningful, not gibberish, he is relying on a *non-relativist* concept of truth shared by himself and the reader. (All writing, all speech, all communication implicitly does this.) Otherwise we cannot understand it, much less agree with him. And if there *is* a common truth then, presumably, the university could educate us in just that. He is not really talking about 'truth' at all, but recording the obvious fact that there is a great variety of attitudes amongst the members of a university to what happens there. And although this is important, it has nothing to do with 'truth' and the problems of knowledge.

Applied to the analysis of educational practice, relativism produces such gems as the following: '. . . the rules of logic . . . are conventional, and will be shaped and selected in accordance with the purpose of the discourse'.[1] There is no comment adequate to a statement like that. The mind spins. And here is fore-

[1] Quoted in M. F. D. Young (ed.), *Knowledge and Control*, Collier Macmillan, 1971, p. 5.

shadowed the end of all examinations, and the concept of academic standards:

> 'One can . . . see . . . research possibilities . . . which might examine . . . the process of negotiation between examiners and students about what counts as "a sound answer".'[1]

Ideology[2]

It is easy to see how notions of spontaneity and relativism could lead to support for participatory democracy; but the connection with ideology is not so obvious. Yet the Marxists, the significant ideologists in the academies, have supported participatory democracy almost to a man. The reasons are not far to seek. Since quite clearly participatory democracy will quickly either destroy the academies or permit their capture by a highly disciplined group, all Marxists can use the concept as a revolutionary weapon against the 'bourgeois capitalist' state. For members of the Communist Party that is probably as far as it goes, since there are few educational systems less participatory than that of the Soviet Union. But other Marxists, believers in, say, Trotsky's permanent revolution or Mao's similar doctrines, may support participatory democracy for less cynical reasons.

Ideology is one of the big words, with a large penumbra of meaning. We shall use it to indicate an intensely activist world-view, where literally everything is seen and described in a characteristic way, so that true dialogue between the ideologist and one outside the circle is impossible. Here is the key text of modern ideologies: 'Philosophers have only interpreted the world in various ways. The point is to change it.'[3] Being what they are, humans live in a world of meanings, and so the most effective way to change the world is to capture people's minds. This is the function

[1] *Ibid.*, p. 5.

[2] K. R. Minogue, *op.cit.*

[3] Karl Marx, *Theses on Feuerbach*, 1845.

of ideology. There always have been ideologies, but our age is notable for the number and virulence of them: minor ones like Scientology; major ones like Nationalism, Racism, Feminism, Marxism. And of them all, Marxism is the most influential, well-organised and intelligent.

The trick in making an ideology is to manufacture a range of words (or re-define old ones by statement and repetition) so that a deliberate effort at persuasion and enlistment can be passed off as a neutral description. And Marxism, as the pre-eminent ideology, has an arsenal of such terms: 'proletariat', 'class struggle', 'bourgeois', 'class consciousness', 'alienation', 'imperialism', etc. Independent thought is impossible when using these words; the answers are built in from the beginning.

Nowadays the most perfect examples come from China. The following has all the characteristic tones— aggressive menace, the pedantic listing and pseudo-precision, and a kind of dreary caricature of scholasticism:

> 'Concentrate all forces to strike at the handful of ultra-reactionary bourgeois rightists and counter-revolutionary revisionists, and expose and criticise to the full their crimes against the party, against socialism and against Mao Tse-Tung's thought so as to isolate them to the maximum.'[1]

The style of the ideologist is always boldly confident in analysis, and abusive of opponents in personal references. If it gets a grip in an academy it is deeply destructive, since it is a world away from the open, critical, tentative style—where an initial hypothesis may be eventually abandoned—which we have contended is the only style appropriate to an academy.

---

[1] Jerome Ch'en, *Mao Papers*, 1970, p. 121.

3 Attack on Knowledge

To kill a man you aim for the heart, not the limbs. Likewise with the academy: aim for the concept of knowledge, which is the very core of the institution. The central attack is on the *validity* of this concept, with related attacks directed against academic standards and against tolerance, the precondition of all academic inquiry.

The main weapon

An amalgam of relativism and Marxism is the main weapon. The extreme relativist reduces criteria of knowledge either to personal taste and opinion, or to the tenets of the culture. There are no universal criteria, even tentatively or temporarily. This is the corroding of the academic foundations. The dogmatic Marxist assaults more directly. The concept of academic knowledge, he says, is a part of bourgeois ideology. Any member of the proletariat who believes in it is suffering from false consciousness, but can purge himself by rejecting this falsity and embracing the true revelation.

The usual process in some sections of PNL goes something like this: from the very beginning the new student is taken under the wing of the activist staff, and like-minded second- and third-year students. They systematically sneer, argue and threaten him out of any steady beliefs and values which until then gave meaning and coherence to his life. The relativists point out with practised ease the variety of systems of knowledge and belief that have flourished, and still do, in the world. Most young students have no counter to this; they have never before been called to judgement to defend their *Weltanschauung*. And it is a People's Court, where all take part. The emotional pressure is intense, however crude, superficial and ignorant the attacks. Few indeed are the students who have the courage, knowledge and intelligence to stand up against it.

The Marxist attacks also, using indifferently a mixture of Marxist and relativist arguments to soften up the victim. Reeling under the onslaught, the student is then given a way out *via* the most rigid and non-relativist structure of all—Marxist fundamentalism. The security of a tight-knit group and an all-embracing world view are offered, and many are glad to accept.

Few students enter the academy able to practise the academic method of seeking knowledge: an open, critical, tentative approach, but requiring a firm commitment to the current state of play regarding what is known. If they leave the academy after three years having learnt this method, then the institution has succeeded in its main task, whatever else it has failed to do. But it is a sophisticated style, steering between the abandonment of criteria of the extreme relativist and the fixities of the absolutist. The academic style is learnt slowly and cumulatively, by the student watching the practice of adepts. The environment, however intellectually lively, should have firm foundations—quite unlike the strident, emotional, conflict-ridden atmosphere that prevails in parts of PNL.

By now there are many source-books expounding the extreme relativist viewpoint, written in the style of the academies but violating the central spirit. Nor is it only in the social sciences and philosophy that the concept of academic knowledge is attacked. The *Radical Science Journal*[1] claims:

'We believe our task is not to analyse science, but to understand society better through analysing the interaction of science and technology with other social activities. This understanding must provide, for ourselves and others, a guide

[1] No. 1, January 1974, p. 2.

to political action . . . For us the concept of scientific knowledge, and indeed the concept of "scientific" itself, is highly
problematical. Within the . . . sciences, it is possible to find
broad theories which serve clear class interests, or which
require underpinning assumptions about the role of man in
nature . . . Indeed it can be held that nature itself is a social
rather than objective category.'

Each sentence can be variously interpreted but yet
the general drift is clear. There is an emphasis on the
social construction of reality, and a systematic ignoring
of the external objective existence of the natural world.
The natural scientist seldom bothers with such trivial
stuff, aware as he is of the immense care, intelligence
and rigorous subtlety of the overall practice and theory
in his own field, and in the natural sciences generally.
It is obvious to him that what is being attempted is not
the difficult creative task of improving, of making
something greater out of what exists, but the simpler
task undertaken by the petty resentful mind—bringing
down the edifice by destroying the foundations. Since
it is so obvious to him, he cannot conceive how
anyone can take such writing seriously; but there he is
wrong. The students have not his knowledge and
assurance. They are much more vulnerable.

An even more thorough-going attack is found in an
article in *Sesame*, the newspaper circulated to all
students of the Open University. Steven Rose, Professor of Biology in that institution, writes:[1]

'Scientists must understand and struggle against the
undemocratic nature of science as an institution (its hierarchy
—all power to the professors: its élitism—all power to the
experts: its sexism—all power to the men: and its racism—all
power to Western modes of thought).'

We expect the academy to discuss with care the
doctrines of Marx, as of any other important thinker.
But this is completely different from the lecturer's use
of the classroom as a forum for propagating Marxism,
either by openly advocating it, or by giving a consistent
and extreme bias to the presentation of views.

[1] *Sesame*, December 1972, p. 16.

Marxist bias

The Marxist bias at PNL has become so well-known and taken for granted that, in a seminar in the Sociology Department, some students stated that they had come to the college 'to create a Marxist cell', that they did not want to be taught anything except Marxism because 'this was what they had come to college for'; they came 'to learn "the Gospel" in order to go out and propagate it'. They seemed unaware that this was a violation of the spirit of the academy. Another student, in her third year, on being asked to consider a variety of sociological perspectives, was deeply disturbed and came out with this *cri de coeur:* 'But we have been taught the truth [i.e. Marxism] . . . if you criticise it, what *do* we believe? . . . We can't proceed with our Sociology . . .'

Here is part of a sober account of this department, written by a first-year student, a young man of unusual strength of character and clarity of mind:

> '. . . As regards the academic environment of my own course, there seems to me a mixture of good and bad. On the one hand there are lecturers of various political shades who have an intense commitment to teaching and to scholarship generally. But on the other there are those who offer nothing but pure dogma, whose criteria for the selection of material are purely political, and whose estimations of the great thinkers of history depend entirely on whether these persons can be fitted into some contrived evolutionary line preceding Marx, or if living later, whether they agree with Marx. For example, one lecturer informed the class that the whole of Hume's philosophy is untenable, although he was not prepared to go into the reasons why . . .'[1]

Moving away from PNL we take some examples from an Open University Course,[2] which may be taken by several thousands of students. Many are school teachers and the course could strongly influence the way they practise their profession. We are told that institutions have the

[1] John Kelly: letter to the Council for Academic Freedom and Democracy (CAFD), 22 March 1973.

[2] Course E 282, *School and Society*, Unit 1, Open University Press, 1972.

'power to structure the realities of . . . people . . . we can feel loyalty towards an institution, we can despise it, and we can . . . feel afraid of it . . . loyalty to "the school" is considered by many head teachers to be a desirable quality to foster in their pupils . . . in the name of an institution we can be coerced, deprived of our freedom . . . punished, or made to undergo severe privation . . . we may even be persuaded that we are not sane; and all these sanctions can appear legitimate or socially acceptable . . .'

There is a clear implication that authority structures are evil, repressive and manipulative. There is no recognition of the benign, nurturing aspects of institutions; instead there are continual suggestions of menacing conspiracy. Mental illness is described in the typical extreme relativist way—merely as a social construct imposed on the victim by the irresistible force of an institution.

Implicit in all this is a rejection of the concept of knowledge as universally accessible and objective. Later this concept of knowledge is explicitly denigrated, by labelling it as 'a high-status thought form', and the term 'knowledge' is re-defined to include *all* thought-forms used by any individual in any society. Further on in the form of self-assessment questions the students are encouraged to believe that 'Learning is not a function of the intellectual ability of the learner' and that 'communication of knowledge is never one-way but always reciprocal'.

Such outrageously 'loaded' statements are particularly damaging to Open University students, since many of them study in isolation, under pressure of time, and tend to take Course Units as received truth. They are thus more intellectually vulnerable than most full-time students.

Attack on academic standards

The same Open University Course attacks the idea of academic standards:

'The criteria employed in evaluation are social constructs . . . supported by particular groups of people who believe in their reality. Through their [examination boards'] management of the procedures and standards of evaluation they give powerful definition to much that counts as school knowledge and school learning.' (p. 91)

Examples from PNL are legion. An Assistant Director of the Polytechnic admitted in conversation that he 'did not believe in academic standards'; he indicated that his rule was to listen to those who made the most noise: the ones who shouted loudest were the ones who mattered. A Principal Lecturer in the Sociology Department, who is now a Governor of PNL, advocated the management of a CNAA degree course by a committee consisting of 50 per cent staff and 50 per cent students, with ultimate authority residing in a General Assembly of all students and staff: 'Decision by majority voting is the seal on the achievement of . . . agreement'. A Vice-President of the Student Union, Peter Polish, stated at the Academic Board that 'all academic standards are political constructs' and urged that Caroline Cox, who had fought against giving authority to the General Assembly, had 'consistently used the concept of academic standards in the Sociology Department to undermine the processes of democracy . . .'

Nor can one rely on the CNAA—although it would seem to be the natural guardian of academic standards. It was this body which in 1971 approved the submission for the above degree and did not veto the clauses which obviously could be (and later were) interpreted to give ultimate authority to a General Assembly of staff and students. The CNAA also agreed to an assessment scheme which had in it *not a single unseen* component.

In the debates on the constitution of the Course Committee[1] a majority of the Sociology departmental staff (as judged by voting) held to positions implying no significant differences in the value of contributions from staff and students in the running of a degree. Also

[1] A body generally responsible for running a course, in this case an honours degree course.

at that time, in staff discussions on admissions policy, those who insisted that student educational qualifications should be checked were openly abused as 'fascists' by colleagues of the Far Left. As one of the beleaguered minority said, the Department might as well recruit the first 50 people from the nearest bus queue.

Attack on tolerance and free speech

This attack comes in two forms: individual acts of intolerance directed against the expression of alternative views, and, more dangerous, active opposition to institutional frameworks (e.g. Codes of Conduct or Bills of Rights and Responsibilities) designed to safeguard the rights of all members of an academy.

An academic inquirer needs to be open and critical, willing to consider all contending views; therefore any attack on the right of free expression of all positions is an attack on the academy. In the wider society there are justifications for some limitations on freedom of speech (e.g. the Race Relations Act); it is much more difficult to justify limitations within the academy. But in PNL there are continual examples of intolerance from staff and student members of the Far Left; and the SU has always attempted, often successfully, to prevent the expression of viewpoints different from its own.

Here is the standard Marxist justification for denying the right of free speech which appeared in *Fuse* 48 (20 October 1974):

> 'If we were living in an ideal society the abstract concept of free speech might have some meaning. We, unfortunately, live in a society where a ruling class depends for its survival on its ability to divide and weaken the working class which it exploits.'

We give a few examples of what this means in practice. In February 1974, the SU passed a motion condemning the Chairman of the PNL Conservative Club for daring to invite Patrick Wall, MP, to speak at the Polytechnic and resolved 'to mobilise to demonstrate its opposition to Patrick Wall, the Monday Club and their racist policies'. At the same meeting a motion was passed 'to campaign against any Zionist societies or propaganda on campus'. Recently the SU Executive have acted as censors by banning the distribution within PNL of one issue of *Sennet*, the newspaper for London University students. They also asserted the right to veto, if they wished, a visit to Porton Down by the Chemistry Society.

The student Socialist Society at PNL have claimed the right to disrupt meetings of other student societies if they disapprove of invited speakers. Also on one occasion three members of the SU Executive, Terry Povey, Graham Packham and Mike Hill, disrupted a press conference held by the PNL Conservative Association.

In PNL there is also a correct line on Women's Liberation. In February 1974, in a series of open meetings, there was a pro-Women's Lib speaker one week followed by Arianna Stassinopoulos (anti-Women's Lib) the next. The first speaker had a warm welcome, but not Miss Stassinopoulos. The Ladbroke House Women's Lib group picketed the meeting and urged people not to attend. They failed to dissuade, so attended themselves in order to heckle. Among the highlights was a question/speech from Roger Hallam, a lecturer, and an executive member of the Council for Academic Freedom and Democracy (CAFD). He wanted to know the attitude of the speaker to the capitalist oppression of all working-class women before he would listen to her. Later, during a heated exchange with a girl student, Miss Stassinopoulos asked her where in the world was there greater tolerance than in Britain. The girl replied: '*You* are the one who counts tolerance as a good thing. *I* don't'. The atmosphere throughout the meeting was oppressive and menacing with continuous nasty heckling.

Outside PNL there have been some notable occurrences during the last three years. At the NUS Conference in April 1974, a motion was passed calling upon student unions to 'take whatever measures are necessary, including the disruption of meetings, in order to prevent any members of racialist or fascist organisations from speaking in colleges'. At this time the NUS also discussed the possibility of issuing a list of banned books, but the national press publicised this, and the matter was dropped. In the summer of 1974 Professor S. P. Huntington was prevented from lecturing at Sussex University on 'The Role of the Military in US Foreign Policy'. Both staff and students at Sussex were prominent in this successful prevention of free speech, and they were subsequently strongly supported by some staff from other colleges, including PNL. Several members of the CAFD Executive publicly defended this act of intolerance. According to one of them:

'. . . it would be a bad thing if every visiting speaker had his meeting disrupted . . . Nevertheless free speech is only one value among others . . . There has not . . . been in England any attempt to interfere with lecturers . . . in the ordinary course of their work . . . I do not think such interference would necessarily be unjustified.'[1]

Opposition to codes of conduct

In late 1973, after some nauseating episodes during one of the regular occupations of PNL, some Staff Governors drew up a Code of Conduct for staff and students, which was passed by the full Court of Governors. The heart of the code goes:

'Preamble
The Polytechnic exists for the education of students and the pursuit of learning. These purposes can be achieved only if its members can work in conditions which permit freedom of thought and expression within a framework of respect for the rights of others. These regulations exist to maintain these

[1] Anthony Arblaster in *Academic Freedom*, Penguin, 1974, pp. 165-6.

conditions, which are essential for the functioning of the Polytechnic as an institution of higher education.

Rules

No staff member or student of the Polytechnic shall

    (a) disrupt teaching, study or research;

    (b) disrupt administrative work, or a meeting within the Polytechnic;

    (c) forcibly prevent any member of the Polytechnic from carrying on his work . . .'

The code does not forbid peaceful picketing or persuasion, nor does it restrict normal trade union activities. But many—both staff and students—were strongly opposed to its introduction. The code provoked the Students' Union to define itself as an independent state, subject to no higher authority:

'Union affirms the need to fight for a strong autonomous Student Union based on mass meetings and direct action. Only in this way can students defend themselves against college authorities. Union states that the only discipline it recognises is that imposed by strong independent student unions at mass meetings of the student body . . .'[1]

The ATTI inside PNL opposed the code on the spurious grounds that it infringed basic trade union rights, like the right to strike.

The opponents of the code need not have worried. It has never once been used, even in cases of the most flagrant and well-advertised breaches. Sustained intimidation has had its effects. Demoralisation, at all levels in the College, is far advanced.

Outside PNL, John Randall, President of NUS in 1974, argued[2] that there is little difference between traditional rag week activities and current disruptions and occupations. The NUS has frequently given enthusiastic support to disruptions at PNL and on one occasion (Disruption 6 in 1972)[3] its President, Digby

[1] Union General Meeting, 6 December 1973.

[2] *THES*, 31 May 1974.

[3] Chapter 1, p. 3.

Jacks, was personally involved. And Professor John Griffith[1] has written:

'I am doubtful whether any useful purpose is served by having a college-based disciplinary system of any kind . . . a disciplinary code within colleges is a natural concomitant of the absurd hierarchic and authoritarian structures which colleges operate.'

[1] *THES*, 31 May 1974. John Griffith is Professor of Public Law at the London School of Economics (LSE) and a CAFD Executive member.

4   Attack on Authority

We have argued that the government of an academy must be built on the concept of academic authority. Those vested with formal authority must be responsible for academic practices and accountable, not only to colleagues and students, but also to the universal academic community, to professional institutes and to the wider society. An academy is NOT a community of equals, and cannot be run as a democracy or partnership (meaning equal representation of staff and students). The justifications of democracy in the society at large do not apply in the special circumstances of an academy.

Attack on academic authority

Although the Director of PNL has consistently advocated government by 'an aristocracy of the intellect', the Deputy Director has repeatedly talked of partnership with the students. Many other staff have also supported equality, with the result that the Academic Board had the highest level of student representation in the country (36 per cent); and some Departmental Boards of Studies and Course Committees have levels even higher than this, rising to 50 per cent in some cases.

We give two examples of the many public statements in PNL which attack the principle of academic authority. The first is from a paper whose authors included members of the academic staff:

'. . . [In social work] the most qualified and experienced have even *less* claim than in other fields to exercise control over decisions on areas of content, method and day-to-day activity . . . Concretely this means that a *minimum* prerequisite for student participation is an equal voice (so that they have a 50-50 chance of winning the point) . . .

'There are two other areas of "responsibility", contracts and external control over courses. But both of these are "obligatory". They are not freely decided upon. If you want a job you sign a contract. If you want to run a course you accept that he who pays the piper will call the tune. You have only the *negative* choice of refusal. Where there is no say there can be no responsibility, except the *practical* one of not getting "caught" . . .'[1]

The paper ends with a set of recommendations which were voted in by the Board of Studies (Applied Social Studies Department), resulting in each course being run by an elected committee of 50 per cent staff, 50 per cent students, with final authority residing in a General Assembly of all staff and students.

The second example is the current SU policy:

'This Union adopts the following as its overall policy on student representation:
1. Court of Governors—50% students, 50% staff (academic and non-academic).
2. Academic Board—50% students, 50% staff.
3. Board of Studies—50% students, 50% staff.
4. Sub-Committee (of the above)—50% students, 50% staff.
5. That all students on the above committees are mandatable delegates and as such are bound by Union policy.'[2]

We have described how the movement for high representation began in NWP. Its success seems to have derived from three factors: the rapid growth of the College in the 1960s with the consequent uncertain institutional identity, and the vulnerability which goes with that; the climate of opinion of the period 1968-70 (the aftermath of May 1968 in Paris); and the coincidence of a mature and skilful SU President, Mike Hill, with a Principal, Saunders Harris, who appeared to make large concessions as a tactic to buy peace.

During the time of the merger with NP, pressures were maintained. In October 1970, Mike Hill stated:

'I have an overwhelming mandate from the membership of my

[1] Richard Kirkwood (Senior Lecturer, Applied Social Studies) and others, 1972.
[2] *Students' Union Handbook*, 1974-5, p. 143.

Union to oppose any suggestions of reducing student representation on any Boards of the New Polytechnic.'[1]

He and his associates were successful. Student representation in parts of the new Polytechnic, notably in the Academic Board, was gradually built up to levels about the same as had been reached in NWP. Ultimate academic authority resides in the Academic Board; therefore any attack on its composition undermines authority throughout the college.

The appalling record of the Academic Board led to demands for its reform. Two of the authors (Caroline Cox and John Marks) were members of the Committee which deliberated on this matter from December 1973 to March 1974. They tabled proposals for Academic Board membership based on the concepts of academic standards and the academic authority, responsibility and accountability of the staff. But they were defeated. The following are summaries of the kinds of argument which prevailed:

> 'To reduce student representation in the Academic Board would generate a response so hostile that the "cure would be worse than the cause".'
> (Dr Leicester, Deputy-Director; and Miss Begrie, Head of Food Sciences Department)
> 'We could continue to live with the present Board and attempt to "educate" or improve it, . . . by giving it more responsibility and allowing it to learn by making mistakes.'
> (Dr Leicester and Dr Tite, Head of History and Philosophy Department)
> 'There are other problems and sources of conflict in the Polytechnic apart from the malfunctioning of the Academic Board; consequently a change in the Board's composition would not help.'
> (Dr Tite and the Academic Registrar)

The ruling principle here seems to be fear, certainly not logic. The style is evasive; there is an unwillingness to face the implications of what academic authority means.

We have argued that natural academic authority derives from academic competence; this in turn is the

[1] From a paper submitted to the Interim Academic Board of PNL.

justification of *formal academic* authority: the vesting of responsibility in individuals who become accountable. Such authority is central to any academy and must be clearly distinguished from authoritarianism. This distinction is rarely made by the opponents of academic authority, both within and without PNL. This pejorative coalescence of authority and authoritarianism occurs throughout *Academic Freedom*,[1] a book commissioned by CAFD and written by Anthony Arblaster. The whole book is a sustained attack on the principle of authority. A few examples will give the flavour.

'. . . students have as much as staff to contribute to the making of appointments and the designing of courses. The argument from expertise is inadequate, and so too is the argument from experience.' (p. 155)

'. . . and I for one see no reason why educational institutions should not be run by a combination of direct democracy and elected representatives or delegates.' (p. 177)

'. . . But in the last analysis an education free from authoritarianism and free from the distortions currently imposed on it by capitalism and the capitalist state, cannot exist within the context of capitalism and authoritarianism in society as a whole. That is why the fight for freedom and democracy in education must also be a struggle for revolutionary social change.' (p. 181)

This is the attack on the theoretical foundations of academic authority. The practical attack is on the working of the organs of academic government.

Attack on the Court

The Court of Governors[2] is the source of governmental authority in the College, and the final court of appeal.

[1] Penguin, 1974.

[2] Our knowledge of these matters is not that of outside observers. Between us we have been elected staff members of the Court of Governors from 1970-75 and members of its General Purposes and Finance Committees, elected staff members of the Academic Board (and its predecessors) from 1968-75 and elected members of one of its main committees. We have also been Branch officers of the two largest ATTI branches in PNL and of the PNL ATTI Co-ordinating Committee from 1968 until resigning from the ATTI in mid-1973; we are now members of the APT. We have participated actively in these bodies in an effort to remedy the situation through the formal structures within the Polytechnic.

Therefore it had to be broken down, to be systematically emasculated and its impotence then revealed for all to see. The destroyers have been completely successful; it is now as personally degrading to sit through a meeting of the Court of Governors as it has always been with the Academic Board.

This success must be explained. To the experienced observer it would have been obvious that the Academic Board was doomed from the start, because of its composition: 36 per cent students, most of them responsive to a Students' Union with a revolutionary socialist Executive. If the students vote *en bloc*—as they usually do—they need only a few sympathisers and/or abstainers amongst the staff to win a majority. But on the Court of Governors student representation is low (two out of a total of more than 30). To win a vote they need large support.

They have been given it on a number of significant issues: by some academic staff Governors and, more surprisingly, by some of the external Governors, notably Professor Le Fevre, appointed by the University of London; and Mrs Chaplin, a Labour Party stalwart appointed by the ILEA, which foots the annual bill of several million pounds for running the College. However shameless, misleading or breathtakingly cynical the speech from Terry Povey, he could frequently count on the open support of these two external Governors and the votes of others.

The Court has 12 internal members: eight elected staff, two students (Union President and one other), the Director and the Deputy Director. There are 20 lay (external) Governors, including five appointed by the ILEA. This was quite a different Court from those of the two original colleges, which contained no internal members apart from the Head of the College. At NWP, for example, a meeting of the Court was an urbane, civilised affair. Unfortunately, its deliberations were largely irrelevant to the running of the College. Contentious matters seldom occurred. There were no established factions, voting was rare, and dirty linen was never washed in public. It was an occasion for self-congratulation, as the Principal of the College smoothly guided them through the mysteries of the agenda. The worthy Governors could return home well content with their afternoon of unpaid public service. Many of the lay Governors lamented the passing of those days and were entirely unprepared for the relentless warfare and the monotonously fixed positions of many of the internal Governors of PNL and some of the newer lay Governors.

The proceedings of the new Court were at first circumspect; but all changed when Terence Miller was appointed Director. Terry Povey and Mike Hill went 'over the top' and things were never the same again. Many lay Governors did not know what had hit them— often did not want to know—and behaved as if the ugly realities of PNL would disappear if they did not look. This may explain part of the absenteeism from key meetings, and certainly explains the resentment of some lay members towards staff Governors who tried to enlighten them on the facts of the situations, either in speeches at Court meetings or in documents circulated beforehand.

Failures of the Court

The failures of the Court are legion. We describe four of the most significant ones.

1. *The working of the Academic Board*. The Director first reported its deficiencies in June 1972. The Court, in its wisdom, decided to wait for the Academic Board to report on itself. Finally, the CNAA reported on it— very unfavourably. Then the ILEA stepped in, but its performance, as we shall see, turned out to be almost as timorous as the Court's would have been.

2. *The Jenkins Affair*. This was the *cause célèbre* of the College. There is a history to it which antedates by

some years Mr Miller's appointment as Director. Mr Jenkins has a philosophy of education: he believes in high levels of student participation, he appears to think little of assessments, he demands almost complete autonomy for his Department, and he is an indefatigable and prominent member of the ATTI. He was promoted to his post as Head of the Department of Business Studies by the Governors of NWP, who at first refused to appoint him, but were 'forced' to do so by Mike Hill and the NWP SU. Mike Hill boasted of this in an election manifesto.

A clash between Mr Jenkins and the Director was inevitable. It centred finally on academic standards and assessment. In July 1972 the Director suspended Mr Jenkins from his position as Head of Department. The letter of suspension contained many points, but the key sentence was:

'In particular, and especially in view of previous DES reports, I am uneasy about the way in which the HNC and HND and endorsement examination procedures are being carried out.'

Normally the Academic Board or Senate of an academy would deal with such a question, but the shambles which was the PNL Academic Board would have been incapable of handling it. There was the expected uproar at the Director's action, the inevitable student occupation, and the appointment of an independent, expert, external inquiry into 'The Running of the Department of Business Studies'. After three months spent hearing evidence, the committee of inquiry presented their report to the Court of Governors in late November 1972. On the main point, examination procedures, they reported in detail, and even the bland, veiled prose characteristic of a committee cannot quite mask the blatancy of the violations which had been occurring. We select a few quotations:

Examinations Procedures
Students in general follow courses of study governed by regulations prescribed by the Joint Committee for National Awards in Business Studies (known as Rules 124) . . .

We are satisfied that there have been serious irregularities in the preparation of returns submitted to the Joint Committee. It is clear that no student has been penalised as a result of these irregularities.'

They then criticise severely each of the four elements of the assessment scheme:

'Extended Essays
These essays . . . were not produced by Sandwich course students . . . in the last two sessions, although for 1971 "Extended Essay Marks" were submitted to the Joint Committee . . . Mr Jenkins informed us that "we do not have an extended essay in our scheme", but Rules 124 explicitly refer to the Extended Essay as "a compulsory element in all courses".'

'Homework and Course Work Marks
These marks [account] for 30% of the aggregate mark . . . in a significant number of cases marks submitted to the Joint Committee differed from those produced by the subject teacher. Adjustments, sometimes very considerable, were made . . . Some witnesses [i e. lecturers] stated that these adjustments were made either without their knowledge or against their wishes . . .'

'Examination Marks
There was some evidence of marks for final examinations being raised against the wishes of the College examiner . . .'

'Attendance Statistics
Rules 124 lay down minimum attendance requirements . . . It appears that where individual teachers did produce attendance figures, these were not used and it is claimed that in some instances figures submitted to the Joint Committee were quite unjustified . . .'

To the astonishment of many, the Governors decided to leave Mr Jenkins as Head but to appoint a Supervisory Committee to oversee the work of the Department. The whole affair developed into a trial of strength against the Director, with the Deputy Director, Dr Tite, Mrs Chaplin and Professor Le Fevre as Mr Jenkins's most effective allies.

At a later meeting the then Chairman of the Court, Mr Brian Roberts, referred with dry disgust to the 'malpractices reported by the Committee of Inquiry'. Professor Le Fevre jumped to his feet. He was 'shocked'.

He violently disputed Mr Roberts' ascription. Later he circulated a letter saying that ' "malpractice" implies a degree of deliberation which can hardly be deduced from the sort of sloppiness which the report described and criticised'. Since the report precisely documents just such a high degree of deliberation in breaking rules it is clear we are not in the realm of rational discourse.

On another occasion the Deputy Director put forward his 'revolutionary idea':

> 'Ladies and gentlemen, we can't go on fighting the students. I suggest that we co-opt the President of the Student Union [Terry Povey] on to the Supervisory Committee.'

By now, after two years of sustained anarchy and violence in the College, the Governors were punch drunk, but even for them this was too much to accept.

In spite of the Court's abject abnegation of responsibility in refusing to face the facts revealed by the Committee of Inquiry, the Director tried once more, in May 1973. At a Special Governors' Meeting he tabled a motion to remove Mr Jenkins as Head of Department. He spoke well to his motion, and others were prepared to support him. There could have been little effective opposition since it was difficult to defend Mr Jenkins —his failure to implement the Committee's requirements had been so flagrant. Looking round the table Terry Povey sensed disaster looming up; the vote would go the wrong way. He left the room quickly and returned with the student troops, who proceeded to break up the meeting. Once more there was decision by disruption, the sure and ultimate weapon. This unpenalised disruption marked the end of the Court of Governors as the source of authority in the Polytechnic.

3. *Confidentiality and communication*. Meetings of the Court are closed, and respect for confidentiality is expected of members; but student Governors have contemptuously ignored this constraint. After two years of leaks to the press, scurrilous leaflets, and

abusive and misleading coverage in *Fuse* ('Our Court
Reporter', meaning Mike Hill or Terry Povey), one of
us (John Marks) proposed a method to ensure open
and accurate reporting. He persuaded the Court that
the Chairman and Secretary should issue a summary
of important proceedings immediately after each
meeting, to be followed by the draft minutes in due
course.

But even this reasonable compromise was made
ineffective, largely by the behaviour of Professor
Le Fevre. He harried the Secretary by telephone and
circular letter and several times disputed at Court
meetings the completeness or authorisation of statements which had been issued. While Professor Le Fevre
was technically within his rights, he inhibited the
Secretary from issuing anything except the most bland
and uninformative statements. In effect *Fuse* and the
student Governors remained the 'official' purveyors of
news about Governors' meetings throughout the
Polytechnic.

4. *Disciplinary action*. Only twice has the Court
intervened. In June 1973 the Chairman, Brian
Roberts, took out an injunction to restrain Terry Povey.
This was opposed by several Governors, even though
Povey had by then been on the rampage for over two
years. But the injunction did not prevent the disruption
of the next Governors' meeting by Mike Hill, the other
student Governor. It was Mike Hill's last appearance;
he was leaving PNL to continue his career in student
politics at Birmingham. Early in the meeting he made a
farewell speech in which he pleaded for goodwill,
rationality and compromise in the affairs of the
Polytechnic—a 'statesmanlike speech', according to
one Governor, who applauded vigorously. Later, when
the meeting got down to serious business, Mike Hill
stood on a chair and in a loud voice began reading out
the court order granting the injunction. He continued
for an hour so that scarcely anything else could be

heard. All the while Terry Povey sat back quietly smiling, disclaiming all responsibility.

Then in November 1973 the Court passed a Code of Conduct. This was drawn up by two of us (Keith Jacka and John Marks) and piloted through the Court by staff Governors against initial opposition from Mrs Chaplin, Dr Leicester and Professor Le Fevre. The code has been punctiliously renewed at subsequent Governors' meetings but has not once been used despite gross violations.

We summarise the extreme actions which have incurred no penalties at PNL:

> the 18 disruptions listed earlier (Chapter 1);
>
> the breaking open of the files of individuals, the stealing of documents and the publication of carefully selected elements from them about individuals who are either members of the administration, or staff who have opposed the rule of the Far Left;
>
> the publication of confidential documents (sometimes in the national Press), including information taken from job applications and references;
>
> the publication of libels about administrative and academic staff, and about appointment committees;
>
> the disruption of student meetings, transgressions of free speech, and *ultra vires*[1] payments of Union funds, by the Students' Union Executive; and
>
> 'serious irregularities' in examination procedures.

We consider that the Court of Governors at PNL has continually condoned[2] actions which would have

[1] The basis for this allegation lies in a statement reported in *Fuse* 29, p. 17 (11 March 1973) by M. Rossiter referring to an 'illegal payment' of £200 to the Gasworkers' Union; similar donations have been made to the UCS workers, the miners, the Defence Fund in the Angry Brigade trial, and the Shrewsbury Building Workers' Fighting Fund.

[2] What they have not been prepared to condone is a breach of committee protocol by the Director. In February 1975 the DES invited comment from all members of the Polytechnic on the re-structuring of the Academic Board. The Director replied, giving his personal views, which he conceded were different from the recommendations agreed by the ILEA/PNL Joint Advisory Committee (JAC) of which he was a member. The JAC criticised his action and he therefore withdrew the letter; the DES accepted the withdrawal and indicated that they would not expect further discussion of the letter by the Governors. Nevertheless the Governors did discuss the matter and passed by 16 votes to 9 a motion calling on the Chairman to suspend the Director. Yet many academics, both inside and outside the PNL, would agree with the substance of the letter, which recommended a reduction in the student representation and an increase in senior staff to enhance the academic credibility and effectiveness of the Academic Board.

provoked severe disciplinary measures almost anywhere else.

The Academic Board

An Academic Board or Senate is the supreme academic
body in a college; in theory it has large powers, but
these powers are in practice limited by many constraints. The main internal constraint is that decisions
need to be recognised as reasonable by the academic
staff. Externally there are bodies such as the CNAA and
individuals such as external examiners; there are also
the informal constraints emanating from the 'invisible
colleges' of the general academic community and from
the opinions of all those who encounter the students
of a college after they have graduated. Besides this
there are the constraints of finance.

An Academic Board exercises general control over
teaching, appointments, research, admissions, and
assessments, and allocates the resources of the
academy. Typically the overwhelming majority of
members of an Academic Board come from those with
considerable academic experience, namely the academic staff. An Academic Board of this kind was
assumed by the DES when it issued its policy guidelines to the new polytechnics. But the Academic Board
of PNL was constituted quite differently; and this has
been the major factor—more important even than the
astonishingly spineless performance of the Governors
—in the degeneration of PNL.

It is worth emphasising just how atypical was the
composition of the Board compared with all the other
polytechnics and universities in the country. At PNL,
students made up 36 per cent of the Board compared
with an average of 11·5 per cent for all the polytechnics and 7·4 per cent for the 26 universities which
have student members on their senates (21 universities
have no student voting members at all). PNL was also
atypical in being one of only two polytechnics with

fewer *ex officio* than elected staff members on its Academic Board; this ratio was 0·85 to 1 compared with an average of 1·7 to 1 for all the polytechnics.[1]

From the beginning the PNL Academic Board has been a political rather than an academic body. Elections have been hard fought and a two-party system emerged early. Amongst the students the Far Left were much the best organised group, and they controlled the internal media. Almost all of the successful candidates in the first election to the Board were on 'the Socialist Society slate'.

The first meeting of the Board (15 December 1971) set the tone for the whole ugly and farcical subsequent history. The agenda included a motion of no confidence in the Director; there were characteristically abusive speeches by the students and a close vote (36 against, 30 in favour, 4 abstentions) in a ballot held in secret at the request of the student members. After this debate many students lost interest in most of the rest of the agenda, since it was concerned with the essential academic business of the Board. They kept moving 'next business' in order to reach some motions at the end, concerned with what they considered the burning issues of the day. Then, amidst near disorder, the composition of the important Academic Planning Committee was discussed, although this item was not on the agenda. Its membership was decided, 10 staff and six students, and elections took place immediately from the floor of the meeting, in the best traditions of SU open democracy.

The next meeting lasted 35 minutes. The Chairman, Mr Miller, ruled a provocative motion out of order in that it did not come within the powers of the Board. Mike Hill, the proposer of the motion, refused to accept the ruling and continued to speak. The Chairman closed the meeting. After the closure a rump meeting was held—all the students plus radical (i.e. anti-Miller)

[1] C. Cox and J. Marks, 'Student Representation in Polytechnics', *Universities Quarterly*, Spring 1975.

staff—and a 'Red Letter' was issued condemning the despotic chairmanship of the Director.

Early in the succeeding meeting there was a long wrangle over the accuracy of the minutes. Finally, a staff member proposed that a tape-recording be kept of proceedings. This was too much for the minute secretary. He got up and roundly abused everybody: the Board was a shambles, there was no order, everybody talked at once, and it was nearly impossible to take minutes. He said he would resign forthwith, raged out of the room shouting 'A happy Ash Wednesday to you all' (for so it was), and slammed the door.

And on it went, the whole dreary, dirty business.

Role of the Academic Board

Clearly we are seeing people act out conflicting ideas about what an Academic Board should be. The conflict has been between three largely incompatible models. We have already described the 'academic' model: the Board as an expert body deliberating on academic matters within multiple constraints, and composed of members sensitive to these constraints.

The radical students, however, see the Academic Board as a kind of Parliament of the Polytechnic, near-autonomous and operating like most student unions, that is, a body under almost no external constraints, which can order its affairs as it pleases and which, unlike the national Parliament, does not have actually to do anything or ultimately face the consequences of its actions. (Most student unions are academically parasitic — they contribute virtually nothing to the academic life of the institution.)

Another important model is the ATTI union model. This ignores the dual nature of academic staff organisations—the tension between the professional responsibility of individuals and the collective solidarity of a trade union. It posits the Staff Union as the major force on the Board. Staff Union members are expected to speak and vote according to previously decided Union policy, to support Union candidates, and generally surrender individual judgement. The guiding principle is solidarity. At PNL supporters of the Students' Union and Staff Union models have usually, but not always, worked together in opposition to supporters of the traditional academic model.

The existence of these competing conceptions has led to polarisation, and a shift from academic to political activity. There is the demanding and delicate business of arranging 'slates' in the various elections. Although some of the 'academics' have shown themselves under pressure to be even better political organisers than the Far Left, they resent being forced to spend time this way, especially as there seems no natural end to the activity, the majorities achieved being so fragile.

Genuine debate has been stifled since the middle ground has been swept away. Academic arguments have seldom been used; the criteria for decisions are party-political. Apart from the frequent disruptions, much time has been lost in futile debates on procedure, in attacking the Director, or in discussing topics over which the Board has no control (e.g. student grants). Important matters have not been raised at the Board, and many staff have been glad of this, having no faith in the Board's capacities. Other matters have remained in limbo for years, having been referred back and forth between the Board and its committees (e.g. staff appointment procedures and the powers of Course Committees).

The ILEA and the JAC

We have already referred to the internal efforts to reform the Academic Board. These attempts followed the CNAA report in June 1973 which was severely critical of the institutional shortcomings of PNL, and especially of its Academic Board. In late 1973 the

ILEA stepped in. A Joint Advisory Committee (JAC) was set up, consisting of the 'top brass' of PNL plus an equal number from ILEA. The chairman was Jack Straw, head of the ILEA sub-committee for higher education. The ILEA issued an ominous statement saying, in effect, that if PNL did not come to its senses and quickly mend its way it might be shut down. Many of the academic staff were pleased that someone else was going to take responsibility. PNL had proved incapable of getting out of the appalling mess it was in; but perhaps the powers-that-be from outside could do the job.

Their faith was misplaced. The JAC met many times, received written and verbal evidence, handed down sonorous statements to the multitude and finally, after seven months, delivered itself of a preliminary report which was a pusillanimous compromise, empty of principle or *rationale*. On the key issue—reform of the Academic Board—they proposed a total Board of 43: nine students, seven *ex officio* members, 24 elected staff, and three co-opted. No academic arguments were given to justify this bizarre and wildly atypical composition: no *ex officio* Heads of Department, still the highest student representation in the country (21 per cent), and the lowest ratio of *ex officio* to elected staff (0·29 to 1).

Jack Straw's justification for the 21 per cent was that it would still leave PNL at the top of the league in student representation. No justification was given for the extreme proportion of elected staff, far higher than on the old Board and as if designed to keep the College's political warfare up to its customary level of destructive intensity.

The ATTI and the SU jointly attacked the report— the slogan was 'no cuts in representation'. When the major committees of the Academic Board discussed the report, moves to increase the student representation were led by the Deputy Director and an Assistant Director, Dr Singer, both of them members of the JAC, which had claimed to have issued a *unanimous* report. At this same meeting the other Assistant Director, Mr T. Roberts, supported these moves; he urged the Committee to stop talking about academic standards and went on:

'Forget about these irrelevant academic criteria . . . You must realise it is the political realities which matter. There's going to be open warfare. You talk as if you are in Utopia.'

In spite of all this pressure, the Governors for once stood firm and refused to agree to 33 per cent student representation. This decision led inevitably to disruption—including a particularly nasty break-up of a Governors' meeting (Disruption 17)[1]—and to further protracted negotiations about modifications to the JAC proposals involving Dr Walter Ross, the new Chairman of the Court of Governors,[2] and Dr Singer.

This turmoil and conflict—endless meetings, negotiations, propaganda, violence—was nominally about student representation; and yet the overwhelming majority of students at PNL have consistently shown that they have no interest in this matter. For example, in March 1975, at a by-election to the Academic Board, the two students who were elected to represent the whole student body received *nine votes each* from a total electorate of nearly 4,000. And a departmental student representative gained a place on the Board after an 'election' in which *NO votes at all* were cast. The decision between the two candidates was made by drawing lots! If such an extraordinarily low poll can occur in a college renowned for concern over student representation, then who is demanding the representation and on whose behalf?

[1] Chapter 1, page 4.

[2] Dr Ross replaced Mr Brian Roberts in March 1974.

5   Attack on Legitimacy

Most staff and students dismiss 'de-legitimising' as unimportant, but those who would destroy the academy know better. The academy is built on the principle of the voluntary acceptance of authority, and those who hold such authority must be believed to be doing so legitimately. Destroy this consensus of belief and you have anarchy, soon followed by the rule of those who possess political power. (In academies these are usually the staff and student unions.)

'Denigration Ceremony'

The most spectacular attack on legitimacy occurred with the disruption of the formal Designation Ceremony of the new Polytechnic in November 1972 (now known in PNL student circles as the 'Denigration Ceremony'). A resolution to disrupt was passed at a Students' Union meeting. The wrecking was carefully planned, the most important step being to ensure that the most militant students attended the ceremony. There was a limited allocation of tickets—a certain number to each department—but the Union apparently had ways of getting round this difficulty.

The venue was Queen Elizabeth Hall, and the programme included speeches by the Chairman of the Court of Governors (Brian Roberts), Norman St John-Stevas (Under-Secretary of State for Education), and the Director. Terry Povey, as President of the SU, had been offered an opportunity to speak.

Trouble loomed from the start. Police were outside, but none were in the building. Students shouted abuse as the main speakers arrived. There was ugly heckling of the speech by Brian Roberts, but his words could be heard. During Norman St John-Stevas's speech the shouting from the student phalanx in the audience (about 200) grew deafening, completely drowning his words, although the microphone was on full volume. Before this, Terry Povey had tried to anticipate Mr St John-Stevas, claiming that the designation should not take place. He refused to be silent, and was ushered off the platform by the Director. The sound now rose to a stupendous volume—the students screaming, chanting, throwing paper, clapping, stamping their feet, kicking the metal backs of the chairs.

During the early part of the succeeding speech by the Director, Terence Miller, the hall resounded to the roar of the slogans: 'Racist . . . Fascist . . . Racist . . . Fascist . . .', making it impossible to hear anything else at all. Then, still shouting, the students filed out and disappeared into the Festival Hall, where they proceeded to devour the whole of the buffet tea which was laid out, leaving nothing for those who came later. Even by the high standards of vileness characteristic of PNL it was a ferocious afternoon. *Fuse* proudly headlined it in its next issue and gave a long and gleeful account. Two years later the 1974-5 SU *Handbook* had this disruption as the cover of the booklet: the ugly picture of 200 stamping, screaming, near-hysterical students acting out their version of 'democracy'.[1]

Ridicule and morale

The assault on legitimacy extends from the institution itself to any person who can be associated with it. All who are vested with formal authority are liable to attack, unless they have gained favour with the militants. The attacks occur in almost every publication and speech, but the clearest examples are in the SU *Handbook*. The members of the Court of Governors— the focus of ultimate authority—are always singled

[1]Part of that photograph is reproduced as the cover illustration of this book.

out; those seen by the SU as allies are given favourable attention, the remainder abused to varying degrees.
Among those favoured:

'STEVEN HATCH—ILEA-nominated governor. Ex-Essex University . . . Together with Jack Straw and others he contributed to a Fabian pamphlet entitled *Students Today* in 1968, in which he wrote: "The proper job of the universities is not to unfit their students for life in society, but to teach them how to change society" (distinctly anti-Miller views) . . . Has only just joined the Court. Looks promising.'

'JOHN PURTON—Member of sociology staff and Communist Party who recently ousted arch pro-Miller man Dr John Marks in staff elections to the Court . . . Anti-Miller but has yet to show it on the Court. Should oppose the Joint Advisory Committee's recommendations on cuts in student representation if he sticks to Party doctrine.'

The leader of the 'enemy':

'TERENCE MILLER—Director of the Polytechnic. An incompetent, reactionary and authoritarian buffoon whose lack of subtlety in implementing reactionary policies has embarrassed the DES, and even his closest supporters. Has waged a continuous campaign against his opponents on the staff, particularly the Head of Business Studies Department, and some sociology staff. He believes all sociologists are subversives. Wants to abolish the Students' Union, which he did in his previous job, which was Principal of the University College, Rhodesia. Lacks subtlety. One true love: the army. Wears a paratroop tie for "confidence".'

And two of his 'henchmen':

'C. CHAMPNESS—Head of Department of Law. Was recently promoted to Head of the Law Department as a reward for two years' loyal service to the Director. Appointment rigged (see *High Command*, pages 106-107). He seconded the motion to dismiss Jenkins. The T. Dan Smith of the Polytechnic.'[1]

'C. K. JACKA—"the wild colonial Jackboot". Probably the most unpleasant of the right-wing staff governors. Member of Mr Miller's inner caucus and took prominent part in the unsuccessful attempts to stab his fellow ATTI member,

---

[1] The alleged 'rigging' of Mr Champness' appointment to the Headship of the Law Department has never been formally and publicly refuted. Whenever his name appears in the SU-controlled media—and sometimes also in the national press—readers are reminded of this 'fact'.

Mr Jenkins, in the back . . . essentially a crude, intellectually-barren thug.'[1]

The central administration is also continually attacked and ridiculed. Any error or inefficiency here is loudly and publicly criticised (especially in *Fuse* and at the Academic Board), while work well done is never acknowledged:

'. . . Are you happy that there is a newly-appointed hatchetman in the Polytechnic, the Academic Registrar, who carries out the Director's squalid instructions with the enthusiasm of a thug running a protection racket . . .?'[2]

All institutional authority in the Polytechnic derives ultimately from the Court of Governors and the Academic Board. Each time one of these bodies vacillates, capitulates to pressure, or fails to take a principled stand on a matter of academic policy, its legitimacy as a source of authority is weakened. But both of these bodies have proved vulnerable. Many important matters are not even raised because of the extreme politicisation. Decisions, when they are taken, are tentative and hesitant; and no one has confidence that plans on anything except minor matters will be carried out. Consequently authority at all levels throughout the College is now unstable, and there is an all-pervading low morale.

The comparison made in the Annan Report between the universities of Oxford and Essex is relevant to an understanding of PNL—although PNL is even further removed from Oxford than is Essex in terms of 'tradition' and agreement regarding the 'gravity of offences'.

'The disparity between Oxford and Essex in the gravity of the offences and the penalties imposed could not be more marked. The Oxford students who were expelled for a year had occupied a building for *two hours* . . . The penalties were exemplary—but certainly no heavier than would have been imposed at Oxford at any time in the past. At Essex far

[1] Biographies from SU *Handbook*, 1973-4 and 1974-5.

[2] *Fuse* 20, 8 October 1972: an open letter signed by members of the SU Executive.

more serious offences were committed and the provocation to the University was greater, yet the penalties were in general trivial. If penalties are meant to be deterrents, they would have deterred few troublemakers in the future. But, then, at Essex there is no long tradition and agreement concerning the gravity of certain offences.'[1]

[1] *Report of the Annan Inquiry*, July 1974, p. 19, para. 108.

6 Intimidation

Intimidation has a clear purpose: to win control and to maintain it. The Kray brothers in Whitechapel, the 'heavy boys' of a corrupt trade union, the political police of a dictator—all use the same methods. First, the victim is threatened. If he defends himself he must be defeated there and then. Once established, domination must be maintained by the occasional repetition of violence and the constant reminder of it. Both physical and mental space must be controlled; there must be no chance of escape beyond the borders and no sanctuaries within the territory.

This describes the ultimate, as reached in some modern police-states or in a completely degraded 'total institution'. Intimidation in an academy may seem to be a long way from the horrors just sketched, but the gulf is not so wide as the reader might think, and the aims and methods are identical.

Physical intimidation

On Monday, 18 November 1974, at 2.30 p.m., a meeting of the Governors of PNL was due to be held in the Board Room at Holloway Road. The agenda included one 'hot' item: the ratification of the cut in student representation on the Academic Board, from 36 to 21 per cent. Early on that Monday morning Peter Polish, Communist Party member and Vice-President of the SU, openly handed out leaflets specifying the time and place of the meeting for those who wanted to play a part in its disruption. By two o'clock about 60 students had formed into a mass in the main corridor at Holloway Road, blocking the side passage leading to the Board Room.

As each Governor entered, the Director told him to go past the students and wait in the Staff Common Room, further along and off the corridor. The Governor was allowed past by the courtesy of Peter Polish, commanding the troops with loud-hailer in hand, and the mob hissed or clapped as they were instructed. No one told the students to disperse on pain of being named and brought before a disciplinary tribunal; nor, it turned out, had anyone taken the simple precautions necessary to see that the meeting could go on.

In the Common Room the Governors were told that the meeting would be held in a small inner room. At 2.40 p.m. they filed into this room and the door was locked. The two student Governors were not present. Later they claimed that they were excluded, on the grounds that the doors were locked when they arrived. One of them was the President of the SU, the head of the Executive which *proposed the motion* at the Union meeting which mandated the disruption. The room was small and airless, and there were more than 20 people present. Many had to stand or sit on the floor, an unseemly position for a respectable old gentleman.

Soon after the meeting began there were sounds of a commotion: the students had discovered the meeting place and had broken through the feeble outer defences and into the large common room. There were noises outside, a heavy thud, and the crack of splintering wood as a student hurled himself against the door. Another one like that would have completed the job. Gradually the noise built up: stamping, chanting, banging on the wall, the metal chairs, the big cauldrons and silver salvers in the kitchen. It settled into a steadily growing cacophonous roar as the hysteria developed.

Inside the room the Chairman had to raise his voice. He had not been long on the Court, and this was his first experience of a full-scale performance. He was clearly shocked; his face was grey and his cheekbones stood out. A few of the Governors were calm, but most were worried. This was not what they expected when they took on the job. The noise mounted quickly. By now the Chairman was literally shouting to make himself heard: 'Item number four—Report of the General Purposes Committee'. All crowded in close, the range of hearing was no more than three feet. Instead of quickly agreeing, one of the cooler Governors put his hands to his mouth and bellowed a pedantic correction in wording. The farce went on: items five, six, seven . . .

A side window with wooden louvres gave on to a roof. A group of students had climbed on to it. They tore out two of the louvres and thrust through their power-hailers into the room. The repetitions of hate-filled obscenities came through at tremendous volume: 'Get out . . . You C*nts . . . Motherf*ckers . . . Get out . . . Get out of this polytechnic. Get out . . . We don't want you . . . Get out of this Poly . . .' The Chairman had developed a tic, he was visibly wilting. Finally he gave up: 'Gentlemen. This is impossible. We will call another meeting at County Hall'. (But no meeting was called, at County Hall or elsewhere.)

The door was unlocked and the Governors, once more defeated and degraded, slowly filed out through the ranks of the jubilant disrupters, still high on noise and shouting. So ended a successful afternoon of mau-mauing. They had humiliated the old ones—the hated AUTHORITIES—and were proud of themselves. They had struck one more blow for freedom and democracy.

This disruption had three purposes: to generally discredit the authorities; to prevent or delay the business of the meeting; to frighten the members of the Court and to influence future decisions.

One of the authors (K. Jacka) filed a charge against the main organiser of the disruption, Peter Polish, according to the procedure specified in the Code of Conduct. The Clerk to the Court tried to dissuade him ('Don't make trouble now'). The Chairman also advised against ('It will make a martyr out of him'). The charge was filed nonetheless, but it was not taken further, because there was zero support from amongst those whose duty it is to guide the Polytechnic.

Intimidation by occupation

An occupation is a bigger affair than a disruption; it is a take-over of part of the academy for an indefinite period. We sketch a few aspects of the Ladbroke House Occupation of October 1972 (the Jenkins affair).

The students move in some time after 5 p.m. They come equipped for a long stay: sleeping bags, food, records, books—all their accustomed comforts. They take over key sections of the building unopposed, including the telephone exchange. Arriving next morning, all is different. Just inside the main entrance the Red Guards are stationed—some sitting behind a table, others lounging about. They watch suspiciously everyone who enters, especially the staff. Amongst the Red Guards are some strange faces, presumably from one of the other centres of student activism: perhaps Birmingham, Essex, Reading or the London School of Economics. They are professionals, and go wherever the action is.

Outside and inside the building—all over the walls —are huge posters in black and red: 'Down with Miller', and a drawing of a gibbet with a noose dangling; 'Miller is losing control of his Faculties'; 'Say No to Victimisation'; 'Today Ladbroke — Tomorrow the World'. Outside the office of a staff member disliked by the SU there is daubed: 'Those who build niches for themselves in the present system are building their own coffins'. Whereas the previous day the building was open territory, suddenly there is a contraction, a feeling of barriers everywhere. Freedom has diminished for everyone except the occupiers, who stand about radiating suspicion and menace.

As usual the administration is in disarray. The Director favours a strong line, but the Deputy-Director and the Heads of Department are incapable of a united front. Lecturers are instructed by the Director not to participate in programmes of 'alternative education', to try to continue normal teaching, but not to use force in opposing disruption. Some academic staff radicals ignore instructions and give lectures in the 'alternative education' programme. One Departmental Head acknowledges the occupiers' authority, and humiliates himself by asking permission to continue classes for students who are soon to sit examinations.

'Alternative education' is advertised conspicuously. The topics covered by the 'North London Polytechnic (Occupied Sector), Ladbroke House, Education Collective' include:

'France '68'
'Black Culture'
'Permanent Revolution'
'Perspectives for the British Class Struggle'
'Social Workers pick up what Lawyers Smash'.

A day or two later a broadsheet estimates progress:

'The sterility of a purely conventional academic approach to education came under heavy attack and there was agreement on the need for a democratic structure of allowing for free discussion of all ideas if education is to mean anything.
'It was decided that the barriers which exist between staff and students on different courses should be broken down . . . the starting point for any alternative programme of education must be what the individual wants to learn about the world that surrounds him or herself . . . At the moment [subjects] include karate, drama-groups, women's lib, creativity in the media . . .
PLEASE MAKE USE OF YOUR OWN IDEAS.'

Over in the Business Studies Department, in the Camden Town building, Mr Pratt is temporarily in charge during the suspension of Mr Jenkins. He is singled out for attention in another broadsheet:

'SO PRATT AND HIS BOYS HAVE BEEN INTIMIDATING YOU
(1) . . . Prodded by us the Court of Governors is to meet . . .

on Monday 23rd. Pratt and his boys are worried . . . Their days are numbered and they know it . . . They are frightened men . . . *Don't let them put the frighteners on you*!

(2) . . . The student union has occupied Camden Town and Ladbroke House. Join the occupation: you do not need to black-leg because Pratt and his toughies try to deny you your rights. There is a word they have never learned . . . *The word is SOLIDARITY* . . .

SAY YES TO THE OCCUPATION!
SAY YES TO JENKINS' REINSTATEMENT!
SAY YES TO AN AUTONOMOUS UNION!'

Back in Ladbroke things are getting rough. Having quickly confirmed the triviality of 'alternative education', the main body of students expect normal lectures to continue. Except for a few they have not opposed the Union motion for an occupation, but as soon as it affects them they begin to complain. Neither then nor since does anyone compel them to face the fact that you cannot support, tacitly or openly, a systematic attack on an authority structure and at the same time enjoy the benefits impossible without such a structure.

Conscientious lecturers try to carry on teaching, but there are continued disruptions from roving bands of Red Guards who break in and maintain an uproar—banging, shouting, bellowing out their abuse—'Scabs . . . blacklegs . . .'—until the lecturer is forced to give up.

There was one final-year class avid for teaching. They were prepared for unpleasantness, but very nervous. The lecturer sat on a chair placed before the door. Soon several inquisitors arrived. Through the crack in the door they were told that it was *not* alternative education, it was a seminar on Criminology. If they wanted to disrupt they would have to push her (the lecturer) off her chair because she was going to fulfil her teaching commitments. 'Righto, dearie, we'll be back.' But it took them 30 minutes to find enough people with the guts to do the job. The seminar was almost over by the time they returned and broke it up.

Many months afterwards the leader of the attack came to this same lecturer and asked her, somewhat shamefacedly, to be his tutor. He told her later that the day he led the assault had been the high point of his political career at the Polytechnic.

This is how the occupiers themselves saw it:

'LADBROKE AND THE COLLECTIVES
At the Ladbroke building, the occupation proceeds very successfully . . . a meeting of the Law Department students . . . resulted in a majority vote of support for the aims of the occupation, . . . it was agreed that certain alternative Law seminars should take place within the framework of the alternative education programme. It later became apparent that the Head of Department had disregarded this agreement made between the Law students and the occupation committee, in that lectures *were* in fact taking place. These *had* to be broken up. On Friday 13th (superstitious?) Law students barricaded the door to the lecture room and wouldn't let occupying students in to discuss the broken agreement. The occupiers eventually forced their way in, but the offending students still wouldn't listen and the lecturer continued. Banging on the metal lockers outside the lecture room had no effect so it was decided that it was about time the Rolling Stones should intervene at full blast. The lecture ceased, with one female student running out in hysterics . . . lectures and seminars are continually being disrupted . . . Many of the lectures that should have been taking place at Ladbroke have been secretly taking place at Holloway and Kentish Town buildings, but not so secretly! There are spies about and I know of at least one that was broken up in the Kentish Town canteen. But how many are taking place in private houses?'[1]

Psychological intimidation

Disruptions and occupations are not the only occasions of physical intimidation. Early in 1973 there were prolonged and heated discussions in the Sociology Department on the different proposals for running the new CNAA degree. One plan proposed a 50-50 staff-student Course Committee, with ultimate power residing in a General Assembly of staff and students in

[1] *Fuse* 21, 22 October 1972.

the Department. To push this plan the Far Left students and staff proceeded to create the required majority support.

The student Left drew up an appropriate petition. Just after a lecture, when there was a captive audience, they took over and spoke briefly in favour of their plan. They urged everyone to sign the petition and then established themselves in the doorway so that anyone leaving had to squeeze past. One stubborn student challenged the procedure. They put on the pressure. He said he wished to dissociate himself. OK, so he could sign in the column headed 'Against'; it was 'immoral' not to indicate a stand. He refused to sign at all, but they almost came to blows before he was allowed through. Everyone else signed in the column headed 'For'. The 'majority' was achieved.[1]

In an academy, as in a state, the mental intimidation of individuals occurs in a context of corrupt historiography. Each new event, immediately it happens, is written up and adjusted to the appropriate categories of political melodrama. The pseudo-historians are indifferent to *fact*; they work entirely with an eye to political control.

The anti-Miller campaign of 1971 displays most of the techniques. On 25 November 1970 Terence Miller was chosen to be the first Director of the new Polytechnic. Seven days later the campaign against him began. It was claimed he was a racist, and a motion was passed opposing his appointment until his record as Principal of University College, Rhodesia, had been investigated. (Seven weeks later—long after the campaign had been under way—the report did appear. It was a long piece of blatantly biased writing, and served as a pseudo-ratification of the campaign.)

---

[1] Despite these pressures, at the final staff-student meeting which decided the composition of the Course Committee, only 19 students out of a possible 56 voted for these proposals. One voted against, the remainder absented themselves. Nevertheless, great play was subsequently made of this 'majority' support.

The campaign was run mainly by the Socialist Society of the NWP. It reached a level of extraordinary intensity in January 1971. Day-by-day fresh posters appeared, leaflets were everywhere, speeches were being made. All restraint was cast aside:

'Would you work with a man Saunders Harris refuses to work with?'.
'Miller the authoritarian'.
'Miller the racist'.

This extract from a later leaflet is typical:

'There is a clear moral issue involved in Professor Miller's appointment. If he is allowed to take up his position without opposition, we, the students, are actually telling the world, "We don't care what happened in Rhodesia. We don't care what happens to black people. We don't care about racism".'

One of the supporters of this leaflet was Colin Thunhurst, a member of the Occupation Committee responsible for 'Alternative Education'. At that time he was a Research Assistant, but his activities then did not prevent his appointment as a permanent Lecturer, nor his subsequent promotion to Senior Lecturer. First elected as a student member of the Academic Board on a Socialist Society 'slate', he is now an elected staff member of the Academic Board on an ATTI 'slate'.

The administration—very foolishly, as later events showed—chose to ignore the campaign and did nothing to counter the misleading and hate-filled flood of words. The SU was allowed near-total control of the internal media, so that the staff, as well as the students, received almost all of their information from the Union propaganda.[1]

On 26 January 1971, the decisive meeting was held. Terence Miller had been invited, and about a thousand students were present. He spoke very well and rebutted easily most of the charges against him, but he might have saved himself the trouble. The battle

[1] One of the authors (Keith Jacka) attempted to circulate a document giving a balanced account of Miller's record in Rhodesia and refuting the allegations of racism. But the copies were removed before they could reach a sizeable number of people: control of information was virtually complete.

had been won long before. With very few exceptions the students, and also many of the staff, had made up their minds: 'Miller the Racist . . . Miller Out'. The vote was overwhelmingly in favour of occupation. In a college with a high proportion of coloured students, racism was a sure bet. The SU knew that if they could make the charge stick, even if only temporarily, they would win the vote.

In fact the charge was absurdly untrue, as was shown by various letters and articles published in the national press around that time. In the early months of his stay in Rhodesia, Terence Miller's opposition to Ian Smith's policies was so intransigent that he was nearly dismissed. The real reason for the Students' Union opposition to Miller was that his kind of academy was incompatible with theirs. His ideal was similar to that advocated in this book: an institution devoted to knowledge and based on the concept of academic authority, with students participating in academic government only to a limited extent. But the slogan 'Democracy' (meaning 'Government by the Students' Union') is not as emotice as 'Racism'. Particularly at that time, Racism was probably number one amongst the Sacred Topics. And since Miller had worked in Rhodesia and had not been jailed by Ian Smith it was easy to make the charge plausible; although, as we shall see later, sometimes plausibility is thrown aside and sheer fantasy takes over.

The 'Miller campaign' succeeded. Damned on false grounds even before he arrived, and savagely vilified and scapegoated ever since, he has been blamed for all the ills of the Polytechnic. He has committed some *faux-pas* (notably, writing two unilateral letters which were strategically inept, but which were entirely consistent with his concern for academic standards). Enormous publicity, both within and without PNL, has been given to these errors of judgement; no public recognition is given to his qualities of courage and commitment to academic integrity. He has been one of the very few senior staff in PNL who has been prepared to incur intense unpopularity by arguing publicly for the kinds of academic procedures and safeguards which are generally taken for granted elsewhere in higher education.

Forms of propaganda

The main tactics exemplified by this campaign can be summarised briefly:

simplify and distort the local history, adjusting where necessary;

label all the characters as 'good' or 'bad', 'our side' and 'their side';

using the internal media, saturate *all* of the mental space;

keep to the same message and repeat it endlessly.

The formula is entirely unoriginal; what is notable about PNL is the thoroughness, the amount of energy that goes into thought control. The result is that the atmosphere inside the College is much closer to that of a modern one-party state than that of a liberal democracy. Most of the people who work there, both staff and students, find it more comfortable to blur their perceptions of this fact; and since, with few exceptions, they have never fought against the Far Left control of the media, they are also unaware of, or prefer not to know, the extent to which they are manipulated in their opinions on College affairs.[1]

The Miller campaign is an example of negative labelling, of blackening. By contrast Mr Jenkins was whitewashed by the ATTI and SU. His case was simply one of 'victimisation', according to 'An Ad Hoc Group of Rank and File members of the ATTI, representing all Branches of the Polytechnic'. At this stage they ignored completely what most regarded as the central issue, the examination 'irregularities'. In a broadsheet they said:

[1] In January 1973 we published a pamphlet which tried to give a balanced and well-documented account of events in the College to counteract the Far Left's distortions. Many staff and students were grateful for the information but many others were hostile, indicating their preference for peaceful ignorance.

'[The Jenkins affair] is about the basic Trade Union principle that we do not permit people to be suspended on shallow pretexts which amount to the charge of opposing the authorities above him.

'The National Executive Council of ATTI have taken the view that the case is one of victimisation and that the detailed charges are of secondary consideration . . . It is a case of victimisation because Mr Jenkins has been one of the most active and outspoken Trade Unionists on the senior staff in the Polytechnic. It is a case of victimisation because Mr Jenkins has been one of the most outspoken senior staff to disagree with Mr Miller's proposed faculty structure . . .'

Labelling

The simplest and most powerful device of the political melodrama writers of the Far Left is labelling. It obliterates distinctions and blocks thought:

Christopher Champness (Head of Law Department) is 'the T. Dan Smith of the Polytechnic'.

Terence Miller is sometimes a 'Racist', always 'extreme right wing', always an 'authoritarian', and, if he makes a mistake, an 'authoritarian buffoon'.

Caroline Cox is a member of 'Miller's Chain of Command', and her name is linked with 'the extreme right . . . be they private armies or the nazi-based National Front'. Also, beware, she 'appears genuine'!

John Marks is 'the most dislikeable man in the Polytechnic', Miller's 'Chief Whip', the 'leader of the right-wing caucus'.

Of Keith 'Bite yer legs' Jacka they say: 'Wouldn't he look superb in a Nazi uniform?'

In PNL labelling has been effective. *First*, because except for a few individuals, there has been no counter-attack—the labelling has gone unchallenged. *Second,* the labels are so arbitrary, so unrelated to the real nature of the individuals, and so abusive, that most of the academic staff are scared stiff. They are afraid of the lies and innuendos which might be concocted about them; however unreal, they stick. Hence many lie low and are effectively shut out from the public political arena of the Polytechnic. *Third,* the multi-site campus of the Polytechnic turns personal contacts with staff and students on other sites into rare events. With their

Polytechnic-wide propaganda network, the Far Left
are well placed to exploit this. A characteristic response
when one meets for the first time a member of the
academic staff from another building is: 'You can't be
the person I've read so many terrible things about!'

Finally, there is timing. During the first week in
college the new student is battered with propaganda:
the broadsheets, the pamphlets, the speeches from
members of the Union Executive and—most weighty
of all—the SU *Handbook,* in recent years a sustained
exercise in lying and calumny. In the 1974-75 *Handbook* the administrative integrity of the College was
described thus:

> *'Jobs for the "Boys"*
> This last year a number of new Heads of Department were
> appointed along with two Assistant Directors. Two of the
> headship jobs were clearly fixed, those of Mr C. Champness
> in Law and Mrs C. Cox for Sociology. So also was the appoint-
> ment of Mr Tom Roberts. Evidence for these charges comes
> from the Director's files that were liberated during the
> occupation.'

Although legal advice indicated that the above
would constitute good grounds for a libel action,
nothing was done by Dr Ross, Chairman of the Court
of Governors. In fact, he emphatically dissuaded
Mr Champness and Mrs Cox from attempting legal
action or even from raising the matter at the Court of
Governors.

Character assassination
In the issue of *Fuse* of 28 April 1974, there appeared a
long article, nominally written by a radical second-year
student, but containing much information which must
have originated from academic staff. This was a time
of faction fighting amongst the Far Left—CP versus
IS—and the author in his anger is careless in revealing
tactics:

> *'Crisis in the Sociology Department*
> Cox appointed as Head: On Wednesday, March 27th Caroline
> Cox . . . was appointed Head of the Sociology Department.

That this amounts to a disaster for the Department is accepted by most staff and students within the Department . . . a factor in the disaster has been the . . . disorganised muddling performed by staff, particularly by those who proclaim themselves as Marxists. [He refers here to members of the Communist Party whom he considers to have been luke-warm revolutionaries.]

'*Mrs. Cox: a Pen Portrait*. In *Fuse* 27 I described Mrs Cox as a "key wheeler and dealer within the Department". Since she has never replied to that description of her, I can only assume that she considers it an accurate description. It certainly concurs with much of what her colleagues say about her in private. [He does not bother to conceal that staff in this Department denigrate their colleagues to students. Presumably he thinks it is quite acceptable behaviour.] . . .

'*The CNAA connection*
A critical figure is Dr Cannon . . . Cast-iron evidence for the connections between Cox and Cannon is not available. The nature of such connections have to be constructed from hearsay and evidence such as Miller's correspondence, which hopefully and belatedly will be published during the Summer Term . . . [He refers to the documents stolen from Miller's files during the 1973 occupation. Carefully chosen sections were published at the time, some in the national press. Others were kept for *High Command*, a small book about PNL published in October 1974 with the encouragement of CAFD.]

'Cannon was also External Assessor on the Appointments Board which decided in favour of Cox. From the evidence generally available, it cannot be shown there was . . . direct connivance . . . However, we lesser beings are free to draw our own conclusions . . .

'*Staff Reactions* . . . the self-styled Left within the Department has failed miserably. It has totally failed to locate its action where its lecture notes are. [He refers to the fact that the Far Left lecturers use the lecture room as a forum for advocating Revolutionary Marxism.] . . . the kind of militancy which has been used to such good effect by the Left-wing of the Students' Union, has been shunned by the Communist Party lecturers who make up a large part of the organised Left within the ATTI.

'*Student Reaction* . . . It is indicative of staff attitudes that the same lecturers who did not want the Course Committee to debate a policy on essay deadlines and alternative modes of assessment, in March, should have gone into a blind flap as soon as they realised that the apointment of Cox was imminent, and started talking to students about the need for "unity" . . .'

In an addendum to this article on events subsequent to Mrs Cox's appointment the same author goes on to separate the true from the false revolutionaries on the staff:

'Certain members of staff did support the motions, i.e. Frank Pearce, Stef Pixner, Colin Prescod and Tony Woodiwiss, and they could be congratulated for daring to be counted in this way. However, their left-wing colleagues who copped out of their responsibilities . . . deserve only to be consigned to the dustbin of history . . . One of the reasons given to me for the low-key nature of the wording was that "even the Stalinists have to vote for a motion like this". In the event, they didn't . . . The Communist Party lecturers . . . were saying "Don't rock the boat, there are very good proposals going through the Academic Board and Court of Governors". In other words, they revealed a total inability to grasp the differential nature of power politics within the Polytechnic.'

In case the reader has forgotten, the above is a description of life in an academy, not of the tactics for survival in a nation torn apart by civil war. The article was one of several on the same theme.

Physiognomy of hatred

Face-to-face intimidation is the most personally destructive of all. Our first example is a submission by a member of staff to the Committee of Inquiry into the Business Studies Department.

'Examiners' Meetings
. . . I had the embarrassing experience of seeing a young colleague immediately after her appearance at one of these meetings. She was literally shaking like a leaf and told me that she had just been subject to considerable pressure to raise her marks in order to pass students who had failed to obtain the required number of marks for a pass. I understood that the procedure in the meeting had been more like a grilling session for her, especially when she had refused to raise the marks by a considerable margin. I was called to a similar meeting on June 9th and shortly after I had sat down I was faced with a similar suggestion, not regarding my

examination marks but about the homework and coursework marks. The margin in some cases was between 20 and 30. There followed a period of tension and at one point I said that unless I was given a precise order in writing to alter the marks, I would not do so, and asked to be allowed to leave the meeting. There ensued a long period of cajoling, and the use of other methods to try to make me change my mind; I agreed to have another look at the papers but said that I would find it impossible to change the marks to the extent required to pass students and even if I did the whole diploma would become devalued.'

At a Sociology Department staff meeting on 2 October 1974, a member of the College Counselling Service was present. She said that Sociology students who came to her with personal problems often spoke of hostility between members of staff in the Department. After discussion a lecturer tried to silence her by suggesting that a staff meeting was not the 'best forum' for these matters. The majority agreed, but another lecturer, Colin Prescod, was moved to shout out: 'We feel too deeply about our theories, we will rip each other apart . . . we will rip the students apart'. Such virulence is not atypical. A newly appointed lecturer said that after he came to PNL he learnt to recognise the 'physiognomy of hatred'. Within this Department there has been a systematic effort by a combined group of staff and students of the Far Left to effect the transition from an 'academy' to a 'political base'. (Despite this, however, we reiterate that there are staff members committed to academic integrity and students who achieve high academic standards.) We cannot do justice to this theme in the small space available; a few illustrations must suffice.

Initiation by intimidation

Intimidation and control of new students begins from the first hour they enter the Department. To avoid ostracism most succumb quickly. A student in her first few weeks in College was publicly abused in a seminar as a 'bourgeois bag'; she soon acquiesced in the party line.

During the days of the debate over alternative schemes for running the CNAA Sociology degree, several students came privately to Caroline Cox and told her that they agreed with her proposals, but they dared not support her at the General Assembly; life would become intolerable for them. Therefore they stayed away from the meetings.

Another student said: 'There are lots of students who would like to talk with you about their problems, but they dare not be seen entering your room, for fear of being ridiculed: "Why talk to that fascist?" '.

At a General Assembly of staff and students, one staff member (Frank Pearce) alleged that certain newly-appointed staff were incompetent to teach those subjects for which they had been appointed. He was asked from the Chair whether he could back up such serious allegations. He replied: 'You want details? Right, you'll bloody well get them', and proceeded to make specific allegations. A colleague (Communist Party) tried to mend matters by proposing a cautious motion that the meeting dissociate itself from the personal remarks that had been made; but the meeting would have none of it. The motion was defeated: public denigration of staff was condoned.

One of the lecturers who refused to toe the line laid down by the Far Left, trying on a certain course to teach in an unbiased way and to cover a variety of viewpoints, was singled out and unjustifiably attacked in a letter sent to all members of the Department, both staff and students.

At a staff meeting where an important matter was being discussed a certain lecturer remained silent. Questioned afterwards he said: 'Everything I said would have been leaked back to the students . . . I have to face them in lectures tomorrow and I can't stand any more'.

An external candidate for a post of Principal Lecturer told certain staff on the day of the interviews that he had been approached beforehand by two Far Left members of the Department. They gave him warning, told him that if he got the job things would be OK if he went along with them and their group, but if he did not sufficiently co-operate life would be made unendurable for him.

The last word on the power of intimidation belongs to the boldest practitioners, the students. This claim is only slightly overstated:

> '. . . no member of the administrative or academic staff nowadays dares defend the director in public. I think that those members of the NLP Students' Union who have played a part in this should congratulate themselves.'[1]

---

[1] *Fuse* 46, 26 May 1974.

7 Bias and Confrontation

We have described how, in the informal life of an academy, intimidation goes with false history. *Bias in teaching* is the analogue of false history, in the formal classroom situation. Anthony Arblaster sets the scene in *Academic Freedom*.[1] His conception of education 'does not demand from either teacher or students that they conform to unattainable, unrealistic and (in my view) undesirable standards of neutrality or detachment'. The Far Left at PNL agree with this charter for bias: 'I will only teach what I believe in', as more than one has said. And there are many others who do not openly proclaim this rule yet act by it within the classroom.

Violation of integrity of knowledge

We know the difficulties of academic eclecticism and the intricacies of the fact-value debate; but we maintain that none of the tenable positions justifies the behaviour just described, where students are kept in ignorance of the ideas of certain important thinkers, or else the ideas are presented in such a hostile way as to preclude any chance of a favourable response. For example, in the Sociology Department, third-year students have been surprised and delighted to find Max Weber interesting. In the previous two years they had learnt of Weber only as someone who had failed in comparison with Marx.

The Far Left students, too, play an active part. There was a seminar on the Sociology of Education conducted by two 'bourgeois' lecturers (i.e. they try in teaching to present a variety of views). Whenever a writer was mentioned who was against Marxist doctrine there was

[1] *Op. cit.*, p.17.

heckling and shouts of 'He's only a disenchanted emigré'; but for pro-Marxist sources there was respectful silence or purrs of approval.

The group of sociologists in the Applied Social Studies Department are the most brazenly evangelical. 'The sociologists in this department are Marxists. We are all politically active and members of IS', said one of them recently to an applicant in a job interview. Occasionally there are complaints from the students in this Department, tired of the monotonously Marxist bias in their sociology teaching, but there has been no reform, although it is admitted that some Social Work students may be permanently influenced.

One way of ensuring bias is to select the right people to lecture on the central course, thus protecting students from contamination by alternative approaches. A group of staff in the Sociology Department 'democratically' voted to exclude a colleague from teaching on the Social Theory Course of the CNAA degree in Sociology. Two of the lecturers mentioned, Mr Fitzgerald and Mr Pearce, are both members of the Far Left.

'Mr Fitzgerald said that there was a danger in setting up a principle that all opinions should be considered since this would destroy the logic of the course . . . Mr Lobel said that the basic right to have different viewpoints presented in our teaching must not be destroyed by a majority deciding what is relevant and what is not relevant. The principle suggested by Mrs Cox was not an *ad hoc* principle but fundamental. The issue arose out of the attempt by the convenor of the Social Theory Group to exclude him from participation in the construction of a teaching programme, though he had been on the panel from the beginning and had been giving $\frac{1}{4}$ of the second year and $\frac{1}{4}$ of the third year theory lectures on the BSc (London External) for a number of years. The Divisional Committee had asked the convenor (Mr Pearce) to reconvene a meeting that would include Mr Lobel. It took seven weeks to get this meeting and necessitated the intervention of the Head of the Department and, in the end, of the Director . . .'[1]

[1] Extract from minutes of Staff Meeting, June 1972.

Assessment of standards

Attacks on academic assessments hit at the heart of academic integrity. In PNL the clearest statement of contempt for academic standards occurred just after the Jenkins Committee of Inquiry had reported 'serious irregularities' in assessment procedures. A pamphlet issued by 'ATTI Rank and File Members' (i.e. academic staff) included this:

'Anyone with claims to mere liberalism knows that the rigidity of traditional examination procedures is anti-educational. They must be done away with. That Jenkins tried to modify this in the interests of the students is confirmed in the report . . . This "charge" is to Jenkins's credit . . . The report calls Jenkins's actions "serious irregularities" . . . We say they are to be applauded—irregular or not.'

The academic reputation of the college is at risk when there are staff pressure-groups committed to such views.

This issue is becoming more important now that polytechnics are moving towards greater autonomy. Having already shifted from validation of degrees by the universities to validation by the CNAA, there are now moves to confer powers of self-validation on some of the polytechnics. These shifts coincide with certain changes in the nature of assessment schemes, e.g. even an honours degree may have few or no unseen components. Academic credibility cannot be ensured in such circumstances.

It is the *students* who will ultimately suffer, for it is their qualifications which may become devalued. Most of the staff who advocate new examination schemes and applaud 'irregularities' have been appointed on the basis of well-respected and validated qualifications. It is not they who will pay the price of their own ideology.

Violation of the integrity of discussion

The *sine qua non* both of rational decision in the internal affairs of an academy and of rational discussion in the classroom is a broad, balanced base of fact, including accurate accounts of situations from a variety of viewpoints. But on many issues most people in PNL encounter only one extreme and distorted presentation. Such procrustean simplification and calculated bias degrades everyone.

The worst dilemma faces those who are liberal reformers by conviction. They suffer a true crisis of identity. For them, it is a reflex habit to try to weigh situations on their merits, to bring all to mind and balance the evidence. But once the Far Left have gained a certain degree of power, the institution itself is seen to be threatened; the basis of academic values and the very ground of their professional lives is shaken. Reformist criticism then becomes a luxury, because such criticism will be seized and turned to account by the destroyers. The middle ground is swept away and the liberal also is driven to simplify, and to defend stubbornly the *status quo* as being so much preferable to the brutal fundamentalism of the Far Left. Or else he succumbs to intimidation, becomes a half-hearted fellow-traveller and lives out his days in self-contempt.

The middle ground gone, and polarisation a settled fact, the Far Left have already achieved a partial victory. For the stereotypes of the leftist propaganda begin to seem more plausible as the tough-minded amongst the liberals, denied a platform for reasoned public discussion, grimly hold to rigid 'reactionary' positions.

If, for instance, the Far Left succeed in 'packing' a department, it may become dangerous to appoint staff on criteria of academic competence alone. Most likely there will develop a tendency to scrutinise applicants to find those who can stand up to the destroyers of the academy. One also tends to abandon the search for a plurality of views, settling for the cruder aim of ensuring an adequate counter-view. So dichotomy and militancy are reinforced and the revolutionists' prophecy of the inevitability of polarised conflict is fulfilled.

When the tactic of confrontation has sufficiently terrorised the academy, general policy-making is subverted by the pressures of the many who want to buy peace in their time, peace at almost any price. Some of these persons openly admit this to be their guiding rule, while others act the same, but pose as sensible practical men.

The Far Left practise confrontation as a settled policy. They deliberately make outrageous, even contradictory, demands. Since they are not interested in genuine and limited objectives, but only in perpetuating destructive conflict, there is no sense in even beginning to try to buy them off. But, of those whom they attack, few have the insight and courage required to hold firmly to this analysis and to make a stand.

At this stage of institutional degeneration many turn to a 'conflict theory' of the academy, i.e. the academy as an institution in which a small number of groups battles for power, each hoping to win control. As an *element* in an explanatory theory such analysis may be useful, but as a complete guide to the functioning of a viable structure it is ludicrous, since it leaves out the central principle which generated the institution in the first place, and maintains its coherence. It is as if one derived a theory of the physical functioning of human beings by observing only those in the acute stages of virulent infection.

To abandon principle out of fear or despair—in one's private or professional life—is to grow hesitant and stupid. The world becomes arbitrary, chaotic and opaque. And it is presumably this which explains an otherwise puzzling fact: that the breathtaking shifts by the Far Left, from one *ad hoc* criterion to its opposite, sometimes in the course of the same discussion, are so seldom challenged in PNL. It also partly explains why the number of those who have opposed the Far Left has been so small.

8 Manipulation of the Institution

The manipulators in PNL are the Far Left. They want to transform PNL into a political (Red) base, from which to launch a sustained attack on 'capitalist' society. The tactical aim used to be 'Student Power'. Since then ambitions have grown. Throughout the country many young Far Left academic staff have been appointed, and now the aim is 'Radical Staff and Student Power', looking to a more thorough take-over of the institution.

The conflict theory

The *rationale* is the 'conflicting interests' ('unionisation') theory of institutions. In an academy the interest groups depicted are students, academic staff, and non-academic staff. It is asserted that these interests are inevitably and permanently in conflict and that such conflict should be formalised in negotiations between the organised representatives (i.e. unions) of the interest groups. The assumption is that primary loyalty will be to one's union.

Clearly this view of an academy is diametrically opposed to the one that we put forward in Chapter 2. We have already indicated that we consider the conflict theory to be spurious. It describes merely the modifications of the institution as it is breaking down, or when it is in a state of civil war. It is spurious because it ignores the *raison d'être* of the institution, what created it and what holds it together, the 'idea' of the academy—essentially a harmony of interests and a mutual concern for the pursuit and transmission of knowledge. Lord Annan in his report on Essex University had this to say:

'Teaching is not a matter of confrontation but of collaboration; and the arrangements of a university are based for that very reason on collaboration so that individuals are not confused by having to pass suddenly from one life style to another . . . to syndicalise the university would lead to the disaster which some members of staff declared is already happening—teaching students to despise dispassionate scholarship.'[1]

The conflict theory of the academy is not specifically Marxist, but is adopted by the activists of the Far Left because it destroys consensus, and leads to continual litigation and politicisation, thereby making the academy increasingly unworkable. It is tactically effective because it makes use of existing structures, perverting them to destructive ends. Also there is positive feedback: the more successful the Far Left are in creating conflict, the more does the theory become validated.

The strategy is:

In PNL the Far Left have so far completely failed to influence the non-academic staff unions. They have been completely successful in taking over the SU Executive, and often successful in controlling the ATTI.

The Far Left

There are many factions, but at PNL the International Socialists (IS) and Communist Party (CP) are most important. Amongst the students the IS is dominant, but amongst the staff the two factions are more evenly balanced.

[1] *Report of the Annan Inquiry*, University of Essex, 1974, para. 194.

The IS aim to 'Smash the Capitalist State' by fighting for 'Rank and File' control of the 'Mass Organisations of the Working Class'.

> *Revolution not reformism.* We believe in overthrowing capitalism, not patching it up or gradually trying to change it. We therefore support all struggles of workers against capitalism and fight to break the hold of reformist ideas and leaders.
> *The smashing of the capitalist state.* The state machine is a weapon of capitalist class rule and therefore must be smashed. The present parliament, army, police and judges cannot simply be taken over and used by the working class. There is, therefore, no parliamentary road to socialism.'[1]

Overtly they believe in 'open democracy', with ultimate authority in the mass meeting (General Assembly), and decisions made by a show of hands. Covertly and in practice they are quite centralist and authoritarian. This two-faced behaviour naturally leads them to hypocritical actions. Since it seems to stem from a genuine ambivalence it would appear to be a weakness, but so far it has not hindered them.

The main CP theme is the same: to destroy capitalist society. The difference is in style. The CP have always held to Lenin's concept of a centralised inner élite group. Any profession of open democracy is quite cynical and expedient: they take on the colouration of the times. But their main distinction from the IS is their doctrine of the 'constitutional road to power'— working within the system to undermine it (first enunciated by Khrushchev in 1956). They are more patient, more bureaucratic and ultimately more dangerous than their more explicit IS counterparts. The CP member usually sounds like the grey apparatchik he is.

The IS and CP work as partners in PNL, but the occasional vicious squabbles lead to revealing public outbursts. In national student politics the CP and their allies go by the name of the 'Broad Left', while the IS and their allies are known as the 'Socialist Alternative'.

[1] From 'IS—What we stand for', published in each issue of *Socialist Worker*, the IS weekly newspaper.

When the Far Left are *weak* the slogan is 'power to the people', i.e. weaken the central authority, the establishment (IS style dominant). When *stronger* they try to create structures and procedures which are most vulnerable to manipulation. They push for mass meetings, elections instead of appointments, democracy as opposed to authority. When *quite strong* they aim at capturing the most powerful structures. Now the cry will be: 'All power to the centre' (CP style dominant).

The SU and the ATTI are used in order to generate and ratify policy, which is then transmitted to the official structures either internally (Academic Board, Court of Governors, etc.) or externally (Joint Advisory Committee, Inner London Education Authority). The emphasis is on the alleged solidarity of all staff and students.

The Students' Union

All SU Presidents and student Governors have been members of the IS or strongly supported by IS. Terry Povey was at NP/PNL for seven years. For four of his last five years he was a sabbatical officer, full-time, and paid by the Union—in effect from public funds.

	SU President	*Student Governors*
1970-71	M. Hill (NWP)	M. Hill, T. Povey
	T. Povey (NP)	
1971-72	M. Hill	M. Hill, T. Povey
1972-73	T. Povey	T. Povey, M. Hill
1973-74	T. Povey	T. Povey, G. Packham
		(then M. Rossiter)
1974-75	G. Packham	G. Packham,
		H. Tumber
1975-76	J. Rosenberg	
	(President elect)	

In December 1973 three of the above, Terry Povey, Mike Rossiter and Graham Packham, stated their political credo in a signed article:

'We are elected to the Students' Union Executive on a revolutionary socialist platform . . . we are members of the International Socialists Group . . . to the question "Can we have democracy in education?" a revolutionary socialist must answer that under capitalism you cannot have democratic institutions of any sort . . . no institution can be won away from the system by any means other than the destruction of the system itself.

For us, therefore, representation is a tactic, not a solution, and use of it must not be allowed to sow the illusion that it can fundamentally alter the nature of either education as a whole or what is provided in the name of education at the poly.'

This should be clear enough, but yet the Governors and some of the upper administration still try to buy them off.

Theory and rhetoric of SU operation

The core concept is that of the sovereignty of the 'mass' meeting, which has ultimate power both in executive decisions and in policy making. It also autonomously makes and amends its own constitution. The democratic will of such a meeting is determined by an open majority vote.

Let us put aside for the moment any misgivings about the lack of protection of rights of minorities and other important matters. For such a body to operate honestly *on its own terms* the following are the minimum necessary conditions:

that the executive follow the constitution in letter and spirit and keep the mass of the students fully and accurately informed;

that large numbers of students regularly attend meetings.

We will now demonstrate how these conditions have not been met.

Information: The two significant committees of the Union are the Executive—which meets regularly, proposes many of the main motions, and carries out mandates—and the Finance Committee, in charge of the Union budget, now £68,000 per annum. These two bodies, once separate, are now amalgamated.

No notices of times of meetings, minutes, or reports of any meetings of these two bodies have ever appeared in *Fuse* or the SU *Handbook*, the students' main sources of information.

Funds: The SU funds are *not*, as with a trade union, collected by voluntary subscription from each student, but are automatically paid direct to the Polytechnic by the various grant-giving agencies (usually public money from the student's local education authority) and are then transferred to the Union's account. The annual union capitation fee is fixed by the Governors. In January 1971, at the height of the vicious anti-Miller campaign, the Union officers went cap in hand to the Governors, asked, and were given, a rise from £5 to £12 per student per annum. Later, in mid-1974, between disruptions 15 and 16, they did the same, and were granted a rise from £12 to £20. This rise was at a time of financial stringency when other Polytechnic expenditure was held stationary, or cut back.

The constitution states that SU accounts shall be produced annually, audited, published on College notice boards and later presented to the Annual General Meeting. All of these requirements have been violated. In fact, although the first accounts were due at the latest by October 1972, no accounts of any kind were produced until 29 March 1974. Accounts, when they do appear, are remarkably brief, but nonetheless revealing. For the years 1971-2, 1972-3 and 1973-4 total expenditure was approximately £133,000. Salaries of full-time employees and sabbatical officers came to nearly £32,000, printing and propaganda to £18,000; in contrast, expenditure on students' clubs and societies amounted to only £24,000. As Carl Davidson said, 'Money, without strings, is always useful'. There is a startling contrast between the minutely detailed examination of departmental annual expenditures in the Polytechnic and the derisory over-sight of the £200,000 of public money spent by the SU in four years.

Autonomy: The Articles of Association of the Polytechnic, ultimately determined by the DES, state that 'There shall be established, with a constitution approved by the Court [of Governors] a Students Union, which shall have the power to conduct and manage its own affairs and funds'. The Union claimed complete autonomy, and refused to submit constitutional amendments to the Governors for ratification. The real argument was between the Union and the DES, but it was always presented as a clash with the Director and the Governors. The dispute led to the Union funds being twice frozen by the Chairman of the Court. This produced the expected occupations and disruptions, resulting eventually in a compromise agreement which was, in effect, a victory for the SU.

Over the years the issues of funds, constitution and autonomy have been a potent source of confrontation. Very few of the students are aware of the facts we have given; nor have many of the staff shown interest in these matters.

Attendance at meetings: The quorum for a Union General Meeting is 200, about 5 per cent of the total full-time students. The 3,000 part-time students are disfranchised. If a meeting is inquorate it is reconvened in 10 days and the quorum then becomes 100. For an Emergency General Meeting the quorum is 250. A meeting remains quorate throughout if it commences so. On one afternoon each term classes are cancelled for a Union General Meeting.

Attendances at meetings to initiate direct action are often good (400), and at meetings to call off direct action are usually high (1,000). Other meetings, especially after the first term, have very low attendances and often lack a quorum (less than 200), even when reconvened (less than 100) or when all classes are cancelled. For example, the reconvened Union General Meeting of 22 November 1972 had about 100 present. This meeting accepted the funds compromise, mandated the 'Denigration' disruption, and elected the delegates to the NUS annual conference.

Another meeting, of 22 May 1973, of less than 100 students, passed a motion amending the constitution. A two-thirds vote of those present, i.e. less than 67 students, changed a constitution affecting 4,000 full-time and 3,000 part-time students.

Yet another meeting, of about 250 students (17 November 1971), passed the following highly contentious political motion:

> 'This Union pledges full support for the Irish Republican Army in its fight against British Imperialism, the Orange Order and its armed wing, the Ulster Volunteer Force. Union demands an end to internment, the release of all political prisoners, and the withdrawal from Ireland of all British troops.
>
> This Union supports unconditionally the right of the Irish people to self-determination. This Union mandates the Executive to organise teach-ins, debates, benefit concerts and also to make available the facilities of the college within the framework of the above policy.'[1]

PNL delegates have often been prominent in NUS conferences. More than once these PNL delegates have been chosen at meetings which lacked the necessary quorum.

The reasons for low attendances are two: most students can get most of what they want from a college without an SU, and if they do go to a Union meeting they are so bored, and so disgusted by the tactics of the Far Left, that they do not come again. Yet a differently run SU, with, say, 80 per cent of its sub-

---

[1] *Fuse* 5, November 1971. This remained SU policy for nearly a year. A subsequent meeting, on 24 October 1972, passed a motion—against opposition from Mike Hill—proposed by N. Bennett, Chairman of PNL Conservative Association, stating 'This Union revokes the previously stated policy of the Union which gave support to the IRA'. The 1973-4 and 1974-5 SU *Handbooks* record this interesting episode in political activism by publishing the first motion (of 17 November 1971), but omitting the first key sentence of explicit support for the IRA and by making no mention whatsoever of Mr Bennett's motion.

stantial funds given to student societies and student welfare, could add enormously to the quality of college life for many students.

Manipulative tactics: SU meetings exhibit several features.

(i) The filibuster is used by, for example, introducing an amendment and allowing speaker after speaker to drone on interminably. The purpose is to delay a vote until most of the opposition have gone home, or even better, to pass a new motion later on which reverses a previous decision.

(ii) Important matters (e.g. direct action) are often introduced as emergency business, with no prior notice.

(iii) Enormous composite motions are put with the important clause tucked away in the middle. One of the best was the 16-clause motion proposed by the Executive at the large meeting of 24 October 1973. Knowing that the current occupation would be voted out, the Executive themselves proposed its abandonment, but much else as well. Clause 7 called off the occupation, but all the other clauses were contrary in spirit. Clause 5, for example, read: 'Union mandates the Executive to publish all the documents which the occupation has revealed'. (This was the 'breaking and entering' occupation, when confidential files, including papers concerning a psychiatric report, were stolen. Some of these were later published selectively.) After repeated attempts to split up the 16-clause motion into parts—always skilfully foiled by the Chairman and his followers—the main body of students gave up in despair and passed the motion *en bloc.*

(iv) There is an insistence on decision by show of hands, and a hatred of secret ballots and referenda. Mike Rossiter (Student Governor 1973-74) had this to say in an election manifesto:

> 'I consider myself to be a revolutionary socialist . . . I believe that this Union is a democratic Union and am totally opposed

to any changes in the constitution for secret ballots and the like . . . True democracy is a participatory democracy, with open debate and airing of issues, and a collective show of hands.'

And yet it is the students who demand secret ballots at the Academic Board and the Court of Governors, presumably to enable some of the more timorous or secretive staff sympathisers to vote with them.

(v) The Far Left students are politicians first and students second. They handle the complex Union rules and procedures with practised ease. Baffled by the general opaqueness of operation of the SU, most of the membership give up. They are sometimes willing to mobilise for a single meeting, but not for the long war which would be necessary to produce large reforms.

The last word in cynical indifference comes from Terry Povey:

'The longer we go on disrupting all boards and committees, the less chance the polytechnic will have of meeting the CNAA's requirements. A three-week occupation creates at least a six-week backlog.'[1]

Association of Teachers in Technical Institutions

The ATTI membership in PNL is organised into five branches, one for each site. In early 1971 the total membership was not high, but by late 1972 it had climbed to over 400 out of a possible 550. This increase was a by-product of the intense battle for control between the moderates and the Far Left. A year later membership began to fall, many moderates resigning in disgust from the ATTI and joining the newly-formed rival union, the APT (Association of Polytechnic Teachers).

We estimate the total hard-core vote for the Far Left in PNL to be around 60-70—say, one in eight of academic staff. The proportion amongst students is certainly lower than this. Our estimate that CP and IS and their sympathisers are evenly balanced amongst

[1] *THES,* 19 October 1973.

staff is derived from knowledge of those who do not conceal their membership plus the voting figures at times of faction fighting.

Two views of a staff union: One group, including all of the Far Left, sees the ATTI as a trade union. The emphasis is on collective solidarity in accord with union decisions. There is block voting at meetings, 'slates' at elections; a conflict theory of the academy. The effect is to politicise the College. Academic criteria are secondary. The other ('academic') group regards the ATTI as a professional association; they emphasise the professional responsibility of the individual, who makes up his own mind; academic and professional criteria come before loyalty to the union. Nationally this deep split in values was one of the main reasons for the founding of the APT in 1973, whose aims emphasise its role as a professional association rather than a trade union.

The anti-Miller campaign, followed by the Jenkins affair, split the ATTI down the middle. Polarisation was extreme. There developed a rigid two-party system, with all important votes on party lines. At first the Far Left had control of most of the branches, but the intensity of the conflict brought many of the moderates out of their laboratories and studies, the membership doubled, and by late 1972 the moderates had won most of the elections for branch officers. But these victories were of little use to them since, having lost control of the PNL branches, the Far Left used their contacts at regional and national headquarters to neutralise any ill-effects this loss of local control might have had for them. The consequent high-handed authoritarian action of London Division and Head-quarters sickened many of the PNL members and was one factor which drove them into the APT in late 1973.

Tactics of the Far Left: As with the SU, there is the same hatred of referenda and secret ballots, and the rhetoric of 'all power to the meeting'. The aim is to have the right motions passed, using any means whatever, and however small a minority is represented. The motions are then trumpeted as an expression of the will of the entire membership and are used to influence decisions by the Academic Board, Court of Governors, etc.

As in other respects, the Jenkins affair illustrates best the characteristic tactics. The ATTI National Headquarters decided that Mr Jenkins must be defended to the hilt, and put a senior official, Mr Tom Jones, in charge of the case. The branch officers in PNL, most of whom were moderates, together with all the other ATTI members in the College, were ordered by letter to keep their mouths shut, to leave it all to HQ: 'You will be advised as to what your attitude should be'.

Mr Jones and his assistants visited all five PNL branches and laid down the law on victimisation. But his aggressive tactics did not produce the required militant motions, since many PNL staff knew much more than Mr Jones about the ways of Mr Jenkins, and about the murky affairs of the Business Studies Department. The slogan of 'victimisation' seemed to many an absurdly inaccurate summary of the situation, chosen for reasons of expediency to coerce members into solidarity and without care for truth. After this Mr Jones held an interview with the press which, as published,[1] gave the misleading impression that PNL ATTI members were in favour of militant action. When asked to correct this false impression, he did nothing, but instead attacked his critics for not concentrating exclusively on the defence of Mr Jenkins.

Having lost control of the branches, the Far Left turned to mass meetings of the whole College membership. The tactics of manipulation were similar to those used within the SU. Another device, revision of branch rules, was used to strait-jacket the PNL

[1] *THES*, 13 October 1972.

branches. About this time the London Division of the ATTI decided on a belated review of the constitutions of the several dozens of branches within its jurisdiction. A small working-party was set up, the membership including Mr Jenkins himself, and—remarkable co-incidence—it was decided to scrutinise first of all the rules of the five *PNL* Branches.

There were two offending rules, both of them in the constitutions of the two largest branches, Holloway Road and Ladbroke House:

(*a*) All proposals for strike action had to be put to a ballot of all branch members.

(*b*) Five members could call for a ballot of all branch members on any motion.

These two clauses made manipulation more difficult, and the Far Left hated them. No one was surprised when the working-party singled out precisely these two rules for strong criticism. The same London Division meeting which set up the working-party also praised the PNL students for giving 'such solid support to Mr Jenkins'. This 'solid support' included the infamous Ladbroke Occupation already described.

Manipulation associated with formal structures: We have described student tactics at the Academic Board, the abusive speeches, the contempt for all except political matters, the block voting. It is now very easy for the Far Left to win elections of students to the Academic Board, since most of the students in PNL have lost all interest in it. In late 1974 the College was racked by disturbances provoked by the proposal to cut student representation from 35 to 21 per cent; and yet in the last two years this was how the voting at elections went: in Autumn 1973, 23 votes ($\frac{1}{2}$ per cent of the 4,000 or so student electorate) were all that were needed by a student to gain a place on the Academic Board; total votes cast were 160, 4 per cent of all full-time students. In Autumn 1974 the figures were

24 ($\frac{1}{2}$ per cent), total vote 230. The even lower figures for the most recent by-election have already been quoted (p. 68).

Frank Barrett (Editor of *Fuse*) had this to say recently:[1]

> '. . . when I took over as Editor I must admit I felt obliged to play the tune that the Union was paying for. But . . . the truth was that people aren't the slightest bit bothered about how many students there are on the Academic Board.'

Of the Court of Governors we have said enough. The Governors have shown themselves terrified of the student Left and have bent over backwards to give in to their demands.

Review of Far Left tactics

As their main intellectual devices in manipulation the Far Left use double standards and *ad hoc* criteria—decided upon at the time to handle each issue as it arises. Here are some examples:

- *(a)* There is the cult of democracy, open votes at mass meetings and opposition to secret ballots and referenda. And yet secret ballots are demanded when expedient.

- *(b)* There is the rhetoric of openness in conducting business combined with the practice of extreme secretiveness (e.g. SU Executive).

- *(c)* Procedure is disrupted ('Denigration Ceremony') and yet *in the same week* a violent attack is made on Miller for not showing sufficient respect for rules of procedure as chairman of the Academic Board. Constitutionality is invoked when convenient (even the use of the legal system of the capitalist state!), otherwise there is contempt for constitutions.

[1] *Fuse* 54, 9 February 1975, p. 7.

(d) Confidentiality is violated (e.g. at Governors' meetings) on the grounds of openness, and yet the student Governors voted not to publish the Jenkins Inquiry Report.

(e) At the same meeting the SU passed one motion in favour of the autonomy of a Head of Department whom they liked (Mr Jenkins), and a second motion against the autonomy of a Head of Department whom they disliked (Mr Rossetti).

(f) At an Academic Board meeting Terry Povey blamed the Director for the lack of a faculty structure in PNL, and yet the students, led by Terry Povey, had bitterly opposed a faculty structure for $2\frac{1}{2}$ years.

(g) Ferocious attempts are made to prevent dissemination of any views contrary to the Far Left line.

(h) The Far Left, especially the students, implicitly claim that they can do no wrong, that they are above morality and above the law. Interestingly, most of the moderate academic staff seem to accept this claim. One can imagine the furore if Mr Miller made the same claim and carried out a breaking-and-entering operation on the SU offices, culminating in the publication of appropriately selected documents.

It is appropriate to end this section with two quotations from Lenin, the master tactician and revered teacher of the Revolutionary Marxists:

'My methods are calculated to evoke in the reader hatred, aversion and contempt . . . calculated not to convince but to break up the ranks of the opponent, not to correct the mistake of the opponent but to destroy him, to wipe his organisation off the face of the earth. This formulation is indeed of such a nature as to evoke the worst thoughts, the worst suspicions about the opponent.'[1]

---

[1] V. Lenin, *Selected Works*, English Edition, Vol. III, p. 486.

'Morality is that which serves to destroy the old exploiting society.'[1]

The liberal dilemma

The manipulators have been successful because the natural guardians of the academy, i.e. the liberals, have capitulated. They have given up in the face of the liberal dilemma. Their failure was inevitable in that they persisted in playing the game by the rules, while the radicals blatantly did not. Discussion of the differing categories of staff is a large subject and we shall merely outline it. The distinctions are common to most academies and the categories we use are from the analysis of John Searle in *The Campus War.*

In an academy the 'liberals' are by far the biggest group. But they are also the most confused and ambivalent in their attitudes to authority. In a crisis of academic government they split into pro- and anti-administration. The pro-admin 'liberals', after a period of observation and indecision, see the radicals as a major threat to the values of the academy and of liberal democracy, and therefore swing to the defence of the administration. They have been few at PNL. The anti-admin 'liberals', uncritically swayed by the same sacred topics as the young radicals (e.g. racism), find it too painful to revise the category of innocent youth fighting for a better world. They cannot exchange this for the more realistic but more bitter category of the smug and arrogant simplifiers, or the category of cynical young manipulators. Rather than abandon their original category, they prefer to edit the facts.

Many 'liberals' believe that the administration should always manoeuvre to avoid confrontation; hence the mere existence of conflict is evidence of administrative failure. This gives the radicals both a large advantage and a strong motive for initiating conflict. The pro-admin 'liberals' are compelled by events to learn how to

[1] Quoted in R. Conquest, *Lenin,* Fontana Modern Masters, Fontana/Collins, 1972, p. 41.

think politically, i.e. to consider the consequences of their actions and to realise that in a civil war a gesture against authority may be a luxury they can no longer afford. The anti-admin 'liberals', numerous at PNL, retain their old style and their unexamined prejudices —a reflex distrust of authority, a glamourising of youth, and a predilection for 'progressive' change—regardless of the fundamental principles of an academy. Even if they have private doubts about some actions of the radicals, rarely in the prevailing intimidatory atmosphere do they have the courage or integrity to express them publicly.

The 'radical' staff at PNL are numerous and work closely with the radical students. As in the theory of atomic explosions, so also in institutional politics, the notion of a 'critical mass' is illuminating. The critical mass of activists needed to paralyse or destroy an academy is not large: we guess that around 1 to 2 per cent of students and 5 to 10 per cent of staff is sufficient in an institution the size of PNL. Absolute numbers are more significant than percentages. The 'moderates', the professional committee-men and managers, are active in institutional politics. They are pragmatists: in matters of theory they live from hand to mouth and under pressure are usually willing to do a deal. The 'conservatives' are negligible in numbers and influence.

Routine political activity in an academy is normally controlled by the moderates, but 'crisis politics' have become nearly continuous at PNL and this crystallises in a division along the following lines:

$$\text{'Left'} \begin{cases} \text{radicals} \\ + \\ \text{anti-admin} \\ \text{liberals} \end{cases} \quad versus \quad \begin{cases} \text{moderates} \\ + \\ \text{pro-admin} \\ \text{liberals} \end{cases} \text{'Right'}$$

At PNL the 'left' group is unusually large. The 'moderate' group is small mainly because the institution's committee structure is fairly recent so that there has not been sufficient time for a sizeable group to emerge. Intimidation has kept down the numbers of pro-admin 'liberals'. Since all these factors operate in favour of the 'left' it is not surprising that there have been few counter-attacks. And it may help to explain why no more than half-a-dozen of the 19 Heads of Department at PNL, and no member of the Directorate apart from the Director himself, have taken a consistent public stand on matters of fundamental academic principle.

9 Trojan Horses

Council for National Academic Awards
Unlike a university, a polytechnic does not have autonomous control over its courses. Most of the degree courses in the college are overseen by the CNAA. This body continually scrutinises both the institution and the courses it runs. Periodically it undertakes a complete inspection of the college, usually every five years. The CNAA has great power over a polytechnic, and a submission for approval of a course is an elaborate and nerve-wracking affair for the staff involved.

The 1973 CNAA report on the PNL as a whole was unfavourable. They said they would return to estimate progress in two years, instead of the usual five. Severest criticism was of the PNL Academic Board, but the CNAA refrained from offering clear suggestions for reform. It was notable that they said nothing about the Board's membership. Moreover, during a visit to the Polytechnic, it was stated that the CNAA would not commit themselves publicly on this central academic principle.

The CNAA have made known that, within a few years, well-conducted colleges may be granted the power to award degrees without direct CNAA supervision. We believe that if these degrees are to have academic standing the CNAA will have to proclaim their attachment to certain fundamental academic principles and will need to set down strict guidelines for membership of college academic boards, as indeed they should have done already. We consider that it is a major dereliction of responsibility on the part of the CNAA and contrasts with the behaviour of the Privy Council in regard to the universities.

On assessments, CNAA guidelines appear to have shifted recently from an emphasis on experiment and alternatives to unseen examinations, back to a more conventional approach. Perhaps this comes from a belated awareness of the dangers inherent in their earlier guidelines; in which case one can say that the CNAA should have woken up earlier and have been more explicit when they did.

Inner London Education Authority

The ILEA finances the running of PNL at an annual cost of over £6 million. In the early days the ILEA showed little interest in the internal affairs of the College, even neglecting for some time to fill two ILEA-nominated vacancies on the Court of Governors. This changed in late 1973. The vacancies were filled (one by Dr Walter Ross, Vice-Chairman of the ILEA Higher and Further Education Committee) and the Joint Advisory Committee (ILEA and PNL) was set up. Dr Ross was quickly elected Chairman of the Court, replacing Mr Brian Roberts who had been Chairman since PNL was formed (and Chairman of the Governors of NP for many years before that).

Mr Roberts, although he was a member of the Joint Advisory Committee (JAC), knew nothing of any of the moves to replace him. This event, seen at the time as a left-wing 'coup', was prepared in total secrecy and was allegedly backed by some ILEA Governors, the student Governors and the anti-Miller group of staff and external governors. It succeeded by 12 votes to 11 at a time when two likely supporters of Mr Roberts were unable to be present. It was widely regarded as a political move and led to John Randall, NUS President, sending this telegram to Terry Povey:

'Congratulations on deposing Roberts. Now for Miller.'[1]

We have spoken already of the disappointing JAC Report. A major influence was the Chairman, Jack

[1] *Fuse* 44, 28 April 1974, p. 1.

Straw, a Labour Party politician, not an academic. He is a former President of the NUS who played a crucial role in transforming it into the extremely political body it has now become. A reading of some of the speeches he made while holding that office shows that he had no sympathy for the style of academic government we have advocated in this book. His analyses of academic decision-making were entirely in terms of power. He seemed committed then to policies likely to produce confrontation, and appears not to have changed his views, since it was he who insisted that in the matter of student representation PNL would remain at the top of the league. He is (1975) a full-time Labour Party political adviser to Mrs Barbara Castle, Secretary of State for Health and Social Security.

Council for Academic Freedom and Democracy

This body was founded in October 1970. It is affiliated to the National Council for Civil Liberties and its ostensible aims are 'to defend and promote academic freedom and democracy in all institutes of Further and Higher Education'. The long-serving members of its Executive—Anthony Arblaster, John Griffith, Rodney Hilton, Ralph Miliband, David Page, John Saville and John Westergaard—have been characteristically very left-wing in their published statements. PNL has been represented on the CAFD Executive from the beginning, at first by Harold Wolpe and then by Roger Hallam.

A major activity of CAFD is the investigation of cases where academic freedom and/or democracy has been supposedly violated. In April 1971 Nancy Gayer, CAFD Executive member, presented documents to the Executive which in her view demonstrated a *prima facie* violation of academic freedom by the PNL SU Executive in the matter of the appointment of Terence Miller as Director. She noted that appointment procedures had been correctly followed, and that if CAFD refused to investigate this matter it would look as if it bestirred itself only to protect the Left. Her report was debated and in effect contemptuously brushed aside, for a two-man investigating team was set up; one member was Harold Wolpe, a PNL staff member who had more than once publicly announced his extreme opposition to Miller's appointment, and had supported proposals in the ATTI for a protest strike.

A subsequent CAFD investigation into the affairs of PNL—not into the appointment of Miller—began in 1972. The story is long and involved. We summarise it briefly to give an idea of the dubious and murky procedures, the personal links and the double standards.

The Kelly Phase (from around October 1972 to December 1973): Phillip Kelly was a journalist on *Time Out* commissioned by CAFD to prepare a report on PNL. In a formal interview with the authors of this book, he admitted that he had no previous experience of such investigations, and no experience of academic administration. There was no public statement of the *prima facie* grounds for the investigation, no statement of the areas to be investigated and no open invitation to persons wishing to submit evidence. Effective communication with Philip Kelly was *via* his flat-mate, Tony Bunyan, who was a radical sociology student at PNL and also a reporter on *Time Out*.

Two of the authors (John Marks and Caroline Cox), as ordinary members of CAFD, wrote persistently to John Griffith and Rodney Hilton (successive chairmen of CAFD) asking for information on the mode of procedure in the investigation. Replies were extremely evasive and uninformative, using routine devices for blocking the inquirer who wishes to penetrate the mysteries of a bureaucracy.

The CAFD Executive is like that of the Students' Union in that it has an implied commitment to openness, bitterly criticising the authorities for secrecy, and yet itself operating in a secretive way, holding closed

Executive meetings (no observers), with no transcripts of minutes available for inspection by ordinary members. This is notably different from the genuinely open style of the parent organisation, the National Council for Civil Liberties.

The Campbell Phase (December 1973 to October 1974): Frank Campbell, an 'itinerant Australian sociologist', took over from Philip Kelly and worked in total secrecy. Even his name was kept hidden from all but the Left until the summer of 1974. He based his book, *High Command*, on documents and some interviews with 'several of the leading "oppositional" [i.e. Left] staff and students'. His study was financially supported by CAFD and he gratefully acknowledges the 'encouragement and assistance' of, amongst others, Roger Hallam (Vice-Chairman of CAFD and PNL radical staff member), and Dr John Downing (CAFD Executive member and unsuccessful applicant at PNL for the post of Head of the Department of Sociology— a fact never mentioned in *High Command*, although a detailed account of his interview for the headship is given without any mention of his name).

Frank Campbell's study of PNL came out in 1974. CAFD decided not to put their name to it, but short of this did everything to support and publicise it. The book was undisguisedly partisan from cover to cover, with no attempt at serious consideration of alternative viewpoints. *The Guardian* newspaper played its part by choosing, of all people, Dr John Downing to review Frank Campbell's book.

Final comment: Most CAFD publications imply or assert, without examination, a close and necessary connection between academic freedom and democracy, and this ungrounded assertion opens the door to their dubious political analyses and conclusions. Since it is well-known that the classical theory of academic freedom posits that an academy is *not* a democracy, this bland assumption of CAFD seems deliberate and disingenuous. The symbol used by CAFD on their notepaper is the ever-open single eye, presumably the left eye. There *is* room for an organisation with two eyes to co-ordinate discussion on academic freedom, clearly distinguishing this issue from the entirely different one of democracy.

The British Sociological Association

We have mentioned that Mr Kirkwood, a sociology lecturer in the Department of Applied Social Studies, told an applicant (unsuccessful) for a post that all the sociologists in that department were Marxists, that they were all politically active and members of the International Socialists. This statement, with other factors, led the applicant, Mrs M. Spero, to lodge a formal complaint with the Polytechnic administration. The two Assistant Directors, Dr Singer and Mr Roberts, were unwilling to act and tried to 'cool her out', but she decided to take the matter to her professional organisation, the British Sociological Association. The Committee on Professional Ethics of this body duly listened to evidence, deliberated, and delivered judgement (letter of 14 February 1975).

They criticised the Polytechnic for not making clearer to Mrs Spero the interviewing procedure, but *completely exonerated* Mr Kirkwood:

'It seems clear to us that the discussion of political matters has an entirely proper place in meetings primarily concerned with exchanging information between applicants and existing members of staff such as the morning meeting between Mrs Spero and Mr Kirkwood and Miss Hardy. At the same time, of course, political questions should have no place in the actual selection of candidates.'

This is double-talk by the Committee, because they well knew that Mrs Spero had been rejected after the *morning* interviews, and had in fact never been allowed to proceed to the interviews in the afternoon.

External political links

For the Far Left in PNL the most important links are through the unions. In the world of student politics, both locally and in the NUS, the two main left factions are the Broad Left (CP-dominated) and the Socialist Alternative (IS-dominated). Any student leader in either of these factions has easy access to a nationwide grapevine. In the trade union movement in general the IS are growing more important, especially in the white-collar unions and the service sector. The IS 'fractions' in the unions organise popular front groups which they call 'Rank and File' movements. These are, for example, increasingly significant in education (NUT, ATTI), in journalism (NUJ), amongst civil servants (CPSA), amongst public employees (NUPE), in local government (NALGO), and amongst scientific and technical staff (ASTMS).

Radical social work

Some readers may think that the sordid degradations of academic life at PNL are of only parochial importance. It is, after all, only one out of a host of academies in the country. We shall show the error of this judgement by using as an example the pioneer work of PNL in radicalising social work in Britain.

Students in the Department of Applied Social Studies at PNL are older than most; and they have often given up other jobs to train for their future work in the various parts of the Health and Welfare Services. The departmental courses include one for the Residential Care of Children, a general Diploma in Social Work, a Certificate for Social Workers with the Deaf, a course for Health Visitors and another for District Nurses.

The work these students will do after training would seem at first sight to be very worthwhile, a help to meet real human needs. But the situation is not so straightforward. A debate is raging about the nature and value of social work. The left-wing radicals claim that social work is merely a device of the ruling class to cover the cracks in the capitalist structure, that social workers prevent the oppressed from developing true revolutionary consciousness and from mobilising to overthrow the system. As usual with such arguments there is a valid insight. Some unacceptable social behaviour or 'social problems' may well be altered only by far-reaching changes in social and economic policy (e.g. truancy, or the 'housing problem'). But it does not follow that social conditions are the cause of *all* the 'social problems' dealt with by the health and welfare services. The Far Left are silent about the fact that there will inevitably be some persons who will be physically or mentally handicapped or ill, or who will be described as 'deviant', in *all* societies—capitalist or socialist. The other side in this debate therefore argue that there is a useful place for social work in any advanced industrial society.

How strange, then, to appoint to a department training social workers, staff committed to opposing the very concept of social work itself. Yet this precisely describes the stance of the sociologists in the Department of Applied Social Studies.[1] They have been self-avowed political activists (generally IS) whose ideology is illustrated by the following extracts from Case Con, a national movement for radicalising social work (and a magazine of the same name) which was originated by staff in this department. The extracts show the grossly over-simplified and inflammatory generalisations and the overt commitment to subversion.

'How Should Social Work Courses be Reorganised?
Fed up of Freud? Interested in learning about community work and political action? Was your training designed to develop a radical spirit and socialist ideas among social workers?
Begin work on a critique of social work training. Begin to elaborate alternatives; help build an organisation to effect the necessary changes in training. Come to North Western

[1] They are only a small fraction of the departmental staff, but their influence is disproportionate to their numbers.

Polytechnic, 62, Highbury Grove, N.5 Monday, November 16th 7.00 p.m.'[1]

Prominent amongst the organisers was Bob Deacon, lecturer in the Department of Applied Social Studies at PNL, an intensely dedicated Marxist revolutionary and a diligent Rank-and-File member of the ATTI.

Case Con . . .

The statement of aims includes:

> 'We stand in opposition to capitalism . . . We believe that the first step to the solution of many of the problems facing social workers . . . lies in the replacement, through working-class struggle, of capitalism by socialism. We oppose the use of social workers as tranquillisers and agents of social control . . . We support the democratic organisation of courses with full involvement of students on decision making . . .'

Commenting on the aims, Bob Deacon wrote:

> 'Social workers . . . are merely the price paid by the ruling class for its own efficient maintenance . . . We reject . . . conventional social work . . . We believe that the central task of Case Con is to organise, as part of the labour movement, rank and file social workers in local authority and other statutory agencies . . . We support . . . principled stands on questions like refusal to accept children into care because of homelessness, and subversion . . .'[2]

There are many social workers who are not complacent about social problems, who know that case-work is not the complete remedy, and that both in theory and practice it can be unsatisfactory. But they would oppose Case Con's facile reductionist assertions, which derive all social ills and personal problems from the evils of capitalism, and which look forward to the socialist revolution as the universal panacea.

In December 1972 over 250 attended Case Con's national conference. The circulation of the journal had risen from 1,000 to 4,500. There were regional organisers throughout the country, and the Case Con activists were increasingly involved in militant trade union work. The issue of April 1973 reported:

[1] *Case Con*, Autumn 1970.
[2] *Case Con* 7, April 1972.

'Case Con is now well spread over the map . . . new groups
are beginning to spring up . . . e.g. Norwich, Coventry, Brighton,
Newcastle, Southampton, Aberdeen . . . the Midlands have
six areas now, centred round Leicester, Nottingham, Stoke,
Birmingham, Coventry and Oxford. Supporters in nearly all
regions are making their presence felt in NALGO . . . EDUCA-
TION, ORGANISATION, SOLIDARITY, AGITATION. These
are the four main focuses of Case Con activity in social work
agencies, NALGO and colleges . . . Case Con is the largest
existing counter movement in social work . . .'

Since Case Con were openly subversive of social
work they sometimes encountered resistance. They
called this 'victimisation' and instructed members how
to defend themselves.[1]

. . . on casework

In *Case Con* (January 1973) John Connor argued
as follows:

'Casework is a part of bourgeois ideology, the purpose of
which is to maintain the institution of the family and to
police the "deviants" of society and to reinforce the Capitalist
system. The family is the main vehicle for transmitting bourgeois
values which present its children to the system as wage slaves
for the factories, mines, docks and the various service industries like the Seebohm factories . . .'
'Some examples of bourgeois values are the Protestant work
ethic; respect for private property and authority in any form;
religion . . . marriage . . . the maintaining of the parent-child
relation at all costs . . .'

An alternative policy is called 'Client Refusal, a
political strategy for radical social work'.

'. . . refusing the client as client and accepting him as political
ally has the following merits . . . it helps to speed the polarisation
in social work practice, and to win allies for the movement in
general. It provides the radical social worker with a justification
for the way in which he discriminates within his caseload . . .'[2]

The travesty of the family and the claptrap about
bourgeois values does not deserve the compliment of
rational opposition. But imagine the plight of 'a client',
a suffering individual who has the misfortune to

[1] Case Con *Newsletter*, December 1972.

[2] *Case Con*, April 1972.

encounter one of these social work ideologists, who refuses to help him or her as a client because this will merely be papering over the cracks of the system.

. . . on young persons

'[School] is . . . the institution in which children are first accorded a delinquent status . . . Normally, the social worker accommodates to the "authoritative" view of the boy as "having a problem" . . . at this point . . . "client refusal" could begin to operate, the social worker attempting always to recommend "no action" and denying the ideology of order-in-schools . . . "Client refusal" in the courtroom forces the social worker into the role of political lawyer working in defence of the culture of working-class youth. Strategies for the defence of youth should now be mapped out by Case Con supporters in alliance with radical lawyers . . . Refusing to service the client as client, and arguing politically against the processes that bring him into court, throws up for question the very ideological basis of social control under capitalism. If such a strategy were to mushroom, at a time when the courts are full to bursting in any case, the working of the machinery itself could be thrown into doubt.'[1]

Certainly some persons in authority are too prone to classify young persons as delinquents on slender evidence, and social workers are right to resist. But this gives no grounds for concluding that all delinquents are unjustly labelled; nor does it justify attempts to destroy order in schools or to undermine the legal system.

. . . on mental illness

'The Socialist Patients' Collective fought the capitalist society —the cause of illness—and revealed the function of the Health apparatus as institutions of violence, whose function is to repair human labour power for capital . . . For example, fever is a manifestation of a form of life but this life is again destroyed by the fever. Illness is life, which has collapsed into itself and which at the same time contradicts this. The change from unconscious unhappiness to unhappy consciousness is the changing of individually treated symptoms into a collective weapon against the illness=capital.'[2]

[1] *Ibid.*

[2] Article in *Case Con*, October 1972, describing the Socialist Patients' Collective in Heidelberg.

Ed Conduit depicts three typical Marxist views of madness:

> 'Mental disorder is false consciousness . . . Everybody is oppressed by the capitalist system . . . but some people are not aware of the social causes . . . and are thus screwed up . . . The way out is to accept a "Marxist analysis", whereupon they would cease to be mentally ill . . .'

> ' "Mental illness" is simply a concept of bourgeois propaganda . . . Some people whose ideas or actions threaten the bourgeois order are removed by physical force or coercion to institutions where they are kept out of action: psychiatry is merely an ideology of the oppressors, which serves to confuse the detainee and his allies . . .'

> 'Mental disorder arises out of social contradictions, so any "therapy" must include revolutionary organisation.'[1]

Once more we are given the infantile explanation of all human ills in terms of capitalism; all institutions are depicted as conspiratorial agencies of social control, manipulated by and for the ruling class. There is no mention of the medical model of mental illness, no discussion of those numerous persons whose mental suffering may be biologically caused, and for whom chemotherapy or other forms of medical treatment may have much to offer. Here one sees at its most extreme the Marxists' horrifying indifference to the sufferings of those individuals whom they are supposed to be helping.

. . . on higher education

> 'The Hackney Social Services hierarchy accused David Fane of being "mischievous", "disloyal", "damaging to his team" and "incompetent and unfit to be a senior in charge of a team of social workers" . . . both the social workers and the NALGO branch executive have shown the need and the desire to protest and to organise militantly, but to date David Fane has still not been reinstated to his job. There have been three public protest meetings, three demonstrations, protests from the students and staff at the Polytechnic of North London and as much talk and conniving from the Council and NALGO as one would expect in the Houses of Parliament.'[2]

[1] *Case Con*, July 1973.
[2] *Case Con*, April 1972.

The modern revolutionist in a liberal society demands the right to ignore all obligations, to attack the system at will, and yet at the same time he wants immunity from all punitive consequences. The participation of the Polytechnic staff and students in the David Fane affair is an example of what the Far Left mean when they talk of an academy being involved in the life of the community around it.

Conclusion

Case Con shows the process of transformation of an academy into a combination of political base and community resource. We see how such a politicised institution can affect the surrounding society. This should warn us not to under-estimate the influence of a place like PNL. Its aura of corruption can extend far beyond its own walls.

10 Challenge and Response

We have come now to the end of our tale of PNL, that bitter history of assault, defeat and degradation. Much more could be told, but enough has been said to justify some fundamental questions.

(1) Should our society tolerate the perversion of one of its institutions of higher education into a political base where certain staff and students are openly committed to destroying the society which supports them?

(2) Should our society tolerate the abuse by some staff of their securely tenured, privileged positions to train students for subversion?

(3) Should our society maintain a college:
  (a) where fear, not reason, prevails;
  (b) where grave misconduct and outright illegal behaviour pass unchallenged and are even vaunted;
  (c) where vilification and lies are continually condoned;
  (d) where each year thousands of students, many straight from school, are exposed to an environment of intimidation;
  (e) where political domination even of the staff is so brutally manifest that 'You will be advised what your attitude should be' (and this in a place of higher education, i.e. a place where the concept of individual critical judgement should be central);
  (f) where a small minority holds the majority to ransom;

(g) where a minute and unrepresentative fraction of the student body disburses £68,000 per annum of public money, using some of it for partisan political purposes?

Parallels elsewhere

The ominous trends exemplified by PNL are not peculiar to it, and would not disappear if this college were to be encapsulated or closed down. The troubles at Oxford University during 1973-4 showed many of the characteristics we have already described: deliberate disruption on spurious pretexts, manipulation of meetings, organised Far Left political groups (IS and IMG—International Marxist Group), threats and intimidation, contempt for disciplinary proceedings and a leaflet barrage. In his annual report[1] the Senior Proctor of the University said that it would be 'very dangerous to be guided by the view' that these are youthful excesses which ought to be ignored:

'. . . because there is a small, but important, minority which is determined on disruption . . . whose excesses . . . are deliberate and purposeful. They demand to be treated in the most liberal spirit. Yet they view the principles of liberalism and of reasoned discussion with contempt.'

One student leaflet admitted:

'Our target is those dons who like a peaceful tranquil life, who believe in the community of scholars etc. Direct action, in particular the tactic of occupation, is the only way to get these dons, not to support us, but to attempt to *appease*[2] us.'

The Proctor concludes:

'Never, no matter what the temptation to buy peace and hope for the best, never under any circumstances, should the University make any concessions which will in the slightest impair its powers to defend itself. We found its present powers barely sufficient.'

Thus Britain's oldest university is attacked in the same way as one of its newest polytechnics. Other

[1] 'Oration by the Senior Proctor for 1973-74', *Oxford University Gazette*, 1 August 1974.
[2] Italicised in original.

universities which have been afflicted include Essex,[1] Lancaster, Cambridge,[2] Sussex, London (LSE) and Kent.

The same elements are evident throughout the Western world. Many colleges in the USA have displayed all the pressures and trends we have described—student power and disruption, community resource, youth city—earlier, more extensively, and in some cases more virulently, than in Britain. This is well known and has been carefully documented.[3] The continent of Europe also has its troubles, less well known in Britain but in our opinion more relevant to higher education in this country. Some people claim that the destruction of the academies there—especially in West Germany—has gone further than anywhere else. Rudolf Leonhardt, deputy editor of the (liberal) weekly *Die Zeit*, describes the West German situation:

> 'The *Bund Freiheit der Wissenschaft* (League for Free Scholar-ship) thus explained the situation in the German universities at a conference in Venice in October, 1973: Radical leftist groups had taken power almost everywhere. They were able to do this because the politicians had failed under the pressure of the students and a part of published opinion. The politicians opportunistically submitted to the students' far-reaching demands for a voice in university affairs. The students then used their position in the academic appointments committees to usher Marxists into permanent berths; in this way they could take care of their own, and build a bridgehead of ultra-leftists in the professors' camp at the same time. Where the radical leftists cannot get their own way by misusing the democratic institutions, they do not stop at terror: they disrupt and boycott courses and examinations. They throw tomatoes and harder objects, and they even perpetrate physical violence. Often a professor's very life is not safe any more.

[1] Lord Annan, *Report of the disturbances in the University of Essex*, University of Essex, 1974.

[2] 'Report of the Sit-in in February 1972 and its consequences' (The Devlin Report), *Cambridge University Reporter,* Special No. 12, Vol. CIII, February 1973.

[3] J. Searle, *The Campus War*, Pelican, 1972; R. Nisbet, *The Degradation of the Academic Dogma*, Heinemann, 1971; Carnegie Commission on Higher Education, *Dissent and Disruption*, McGraw Hill, 1971; M. Teodori (ed.), *The New Left: A Documentary History*, Jonathan Cape, 1970.

'The goal of these students is to gain firm control of the universities and then bring down the parliamentary system from there: in other words to begin the "March through the Institutional Hierarchy" that Rudi Dutschke, the most famous German student leader, recommended as good strategy during the student revolts of 1968.'[1]

All of these fears are corroborated in detail in two recent long articles,[2] analysing and describing the activities of the revolutionary movement which flourishes in the countries of the Western world and which concentrates particularly on the institutions of higher education. Within Britain PNL is important not in itself but because it is a microcosm and can be used as a laboratory for examining the strategy and tactics of this movement. Accordingly, we turn to discuss in some detail the ideas and practices of the most sophisticated and dangerous adherents of this movement, commencing with a theoretical analysis based largely on Schelsky.

The long march through the institutions

The strategic aim is to destroy Western liberal democracy by totally discrediting its fundamental values of self-determination, respect for the rights of others, and the rule of law. What kind of society will follow is unclear, except that it will be minutely controlled (totalitarian) and will display a Marxist label.

The revolutionaries' analysis of the distribution of power is tactically effective. They see modern Western societies as protected by a network of institutions which rest on opinion (consent) rather than force. Hence the strategy is to gain control of these institutions one by

[1] The situation in West Germany is such common knowledge there that this article was translated and reprinted in a glossy pamphlet, *Meet Germany*, distributed by the West German Embassy in London.

[2] H. Schelsky, 'The Wider Setting of Disorder in the German Universities', *Minerva*, X, No. 4, October 1972 (Prof. Schelsky is Professor of Sociology at the University of Bielefeld); W. Rüegg, 'The Intellectual Situation in German Higher Education', *Minerva*, XIII, No. 1, Spring 1975 (Prof. Rüegg was Professor of Sociology at the University of Frankfurt from 1961-73 and has been Rector of Frankfurt University and President of the West German Rectors' Conference).

one, relying mostly on propaganda and manipulation. Words, not guns, are the weapons.

Modern man lives increasingly in a world of symbols; he has little direct contact with the natural world. Hence those who are expert with symbols, the professionals in communication and interpretation, have become a large and dominant class. The institutions involved are those of education and training, of information and entertainment—including the cinema, the theatre and publishing; and also the political parties and the churches. Clearly the universities, polytechnics and teacher training colleges are decisive because not only are they themselves institutions which specialise in interpretation, but they also produce graduates who will staff most of the institutions of communication and interpretation.

The enemy is the 'establishment', the 'system', personified by anyone to the right of the Far Left in a position of authority, however such a person has been elected or appointed. Typically no justification is given for opposing the 'establishment': the style is one of pure assertion.

Tactics

The most widespread tactic is to undermine an institution by using its own foundation values against it, and by enlisting as inadvertent allies in this work of destruction persons who are themselves convinced liberals.

When the revolutionaries operate through the liberals they use the method of distortion, exaggerating some elements and ignoring others. For example, British Courts of Justice proclaim the principle of 'innocent until proved guilty'. Many persons from strong moral convictions will labour to change the popular image of the lawbreaker as a repellent criminal into an image of one deserving sympathy. This may be laudable but it does not follow that the judge should be cast as an oppressor, rather than the protector of the rights of others. To achieve their aim the revolutionaries merely have to set up a popular front organisation consisting mostly of liberals, with themselves in a few key positions. An example in Britain is CAFD which, at least in its early days, contained many members who were genuine liberals, although the Executive has always been heavily Marxist.

When the revolutionaries have a foothold in the structure of the institution the main technique is that of the *double standard*. For example, when it suits them they will adhere to a minutely literal interpretation of rules of procedure, while breaking the rules when convenient, denouncing them as legal formalism and a device for oppression by the establishment. Here the strategic trick lies in the tacit refusal to show that readiness for co-operation which is presumed by all rules of judicial and administrative procedure. The man of good will who consistently holds to the rule of law cannot cope with this situation.

Unlike earlier revolutionaries they do not concentrate on *violence*, but they use it in two situations. Firstly, to intimidate opponents, actual or potential—psychological intimidation is usually sufficient; secondly, as an occasional provocation of the agents of law and order, to tempt them into an excessive response, so that the propaganda machine can then depict them as monsters.

The technique of *excessive demands* is pitched at two levels. Demands may be impossible and designed for purposes of confrontation, as when a student union demands that all staff appointments be decided by voting, the electorate to consist of all staff and students. Alternatively, demands are pushed dangerously high and designed to destroy by attrition, as when the Far Left encourages wage demands out of proportion to productive capacity, which will lead eventually to collapse, either of the industry or of the whole economy.

West German model

The tactics have been most conspicuously successful in West Germany. There the New Left radicals have captured many of the universities, and have converted them into strategic headquarters for the revolutionary transformation of society. In estimating the achievements of the destroyers of reason one observer[1] distinguished four types of university:

'1. those which function more or less, e.g. Munich or Cologne;

2. those which are fought over and are in constant danger, e.g. Frankfurt, Göttingen, Hanover, Braunschweig;

3. those which have essentially been "conquered": Berlin, Marburg,[2] Heidelberg, Regensburg;

4. newly-founded universities, which as institutionalised counter-universities have become strongholds of radical indoctrination. Among these are the universities of Bremen, Kassel, Oldenburg and Osnabrück.'

PNL falls somewhere between categories 2 and 3.

One of the first moves after conquering a university is to re-cast the courses for the training of school-teachers, so that they will graduate as revolutionary fighters, able to instruct their young pupils in the art of waging war against their parents, their future employers, and all other representatives of the 'system'. The resultant campaign of child indoctrination is most advanced in the schools of the Federal State of Hesse, where pupils are taught, for example, to distinguish among their classmates the members of various social classes and to choose their friends with regard to loyalties in the class conflict. The Hesse Ministry of Education recently published a framework of Marxist instruction for all subjects. Language-training, for instance, was meant to educate the pupils in the 'class-specific' use

---

[1] Professor Thomas Nipperday, *Deutsche Universitatszeitung*, November 1974, p. 96.

[2] CAFD in Britain has informal links with the Bund Demokratischer Wissenschaftler, based at the University of Marburg; CAFD members were recently asked to sign a petition which protested against the alleged victimisation of academic staff in West Germany. No details were given.

of language for purposes of power and ideological rebellion.[1]

In the universities a complete Marxist takeover is the aim of Spartakus, the communist student group:

> 'We are carrying on the struggle for securing the position of Marxism in university studies, but not as a pluralistic supplement to the bourgeois scientific enterprise, since co-existence between bourgeois and Marxist science within the university is impossible.'

What explains the failure of university teachers in West Germany to resist effectively this takeover of so many of the academies? First, there is intimidation— much the same as in PNL, but more widespread and often more virulent. For years many university teachers have had to work in buildings besmirched with obscene radical slogans, often directed at individual teachers by name. They have had to suffer disruption of lectures, libels, slanders, threats, and sometimes assaults without receiving any protection from the state:

> 'Classes and meetings are made into ordeals by rhythmic clapping, outcries, whistling and by bringing in small children, dogs and other distractions. When this does not suffice [to break the spirit of the teacher] anonymous telephone calls to the professor's wife, children and parents explain what a reactionary capitalist swine the husband, father or son is, and declare that he will soon be brought to account by bombs or similar devices.'[2]

An even more important reason is the university laws passed in the late 1960s, which in many states gave students, professors, and assistants one-third each of the seats on all university bodies, *including appointments committees*. The reader who has read this far will easily see how such laws are a godsend to those who wish to transform the university into a political

---

[1] It is encouraging to record that the Minister of Education suffered a setback. His activities as a Marxist indoctrinator were mainly responsible for the landslide against his party in the Landtag elections in Hesse in October 1974; he was forced to resign.

[2] W. Rüegg, *op cit.*, p. 110.

base. This structure of tripartite government describes exactly the PNL Academic Board, although as yet there are no students on appointments committees, despite persistent attempts to bring this about.

The German laws also gave large funds directly to student organisations which

> 'are spent by executive committees, mostly of the extreme left, for political agitation inside and outside the university . . . The left-wing radicals have thus been provided with a subsidy by the state for actions which are intended to destroy the state.'

Here again there is a close parallel, not just with PNL, but with academies all over Britain.

In 1969 the Communist Party of the Soviet Union changed its line and welcomed the student movement in Western countries as a new instrument in the 'struggle against monopoly capitalism',[1] and in 1970 the Communist Party in West Germany 'began to exploit the opportunities provided by the new university laws and to turn the universities into training centres for communist cadres'.

Inevitably, there has been a fall in academic standards. Some universities outside Germany are no longer willing to accept German examination results at their face value; and inside the Federal Republic some people in industrial and governmental circles are proposing that institutions like the rigorous *grandes écoles* of France should be established.

RESPONSE:
TOWARDS AGGRESSIVE TOLERANCE

Using the latest weapons and tactics, with a realistic analysis and a clear plan of campaign, the left-wing totalitarians are waging war on the academy as a key institution in modern society. With few exceptions the academies have proved inept at self-defence. We offer

---

[1] 'Leninism—The People's Flag against Imperialism and for the Revolutionary Renewal of the World', Theses of the Central Committee of the Communist Party of the Soviet Union, 23 December 1969.

some prescriptions for survival, drawn from experience in Britain, USA and West Germany.

Principles, definitions, distinctions

We have argued that an academy must manifest the spirit of tolerance, of respect for others' views, of the supremacy of persuasion, of concern for hard facts and analysis. It must be devoted to truth and scholarship and its institutional practices and structures of government must accord with this devotion. All serious attacks on the academy aim at these central values and the structures which embody them.

First, a distinction must be made between *dissent* and *disruption;* it is well expressed by the Carnegie Commission Report:

'Dissent and disruption are not simply different methods of expressing the same point of view. Dissent respects the rights of one's fellow citizens; it relies on persuasion. Disruption is based on disregard for the rights of others; it relies on coercion. Dissent is essential in a free society. Disruption is destructive of legitimate democratic processes.'[1]

The Report gives examples of how this distinction may apply in practice:

'Dissent is properly protected in a democracy; disruption must be sternly condemned, suppressed and punished. The border line between dissent and disruptive interference is thus a crucial one and is sometimes difficult to draw. The strike, conducted within the law, is defined as dissent, as is peaceful picketing. A perplexing but common problem of drawing lines is the sit-in. We define it as *dissent* if no one is injured, threatened, or abused; no property is stolen or campus rules broken; and ingress and egress are not hindered. Like the non-obstructive picket line, the non-obstructive sit-in deserves consideration as a democratic means of expression; it may be viewed as a sedentary picket line. Disruption occurs when actions become coercive and obstructive and go beyond the legally conducted strike, peaceful picketing, the peaceful non-obstructive sit-in, and other persuasive actions.'[2]

[1] Carnegie Commission on Higher Education, *op cit.,* p. 12.

[2] *Ibid.,* p. 6.

Policy

Principles and beliefs, to be effective practically, must be embodied in institutional policy. A clear policy which is always acted upon will deter potential aggressors and serve as a guide and support for defenders under attack.

A *Bill of Rights and Responsibilities* is fundamental to the defence of the academy. A model bill is set out in the Carnegie Commission Report. It applies to all members of the academy: academic and non-academic staff, and students. We summarise some of the most important sections:

Rights and responsibilities are divided into

Rights of members as citizens.

Rights of members based on the nature of the educational process.

Rights of the institution.

Rights of members to fair hearings when charged with violation of regulations.

General principles include the following:

Freedom of speech, of the press, of peaceful assembly and of political beliefs. Also freedom from violence and personal abuse.

The 'obligation to respect the freedom to teach, to learn and to conduct research and publish findings in the spirit of free inquiry'.

The 'obligation not to interfere with the freedom of members of a campus to pursue normal academic and administrative activities, including freedom of movement'.

Censorship is forbidden; also secret research.

The institution is obliged to maintain order on the campus, to provide facilities for meetings, but to avoid taking stands on general public issues. The institution must protect itself from abuse of its facilities by individuals and groups.

The institution must specify procedures to be followed in hearing charges against members accused of violating regulations.

Disciplinary procedures and sanctions

A Bill of this kind safeguards the central principles of an academy. If these are violated the academy's response must be intransigent. There must be sanctions—clear, precise, and widely published—ranging from warnings and reprimands to outright dismissal; and they must be used in *every* case of violation. This connects with the appointment and promotion of staff, and the enrolment of students. We suggest that not only should there be regulations governing *acts* against the academy, but also that the appointments and promotions procedure be used to encourage those persons who support the academy and to discourage those who attack and undermine it. At the present time overt criteria depend only on individual academic attainment. These should be expanded to include collective academic criteria, i.e. work done by a staff member to preserve the collective academic framework—showing a positive commitment to institutional academic values—should count explicitly in favour of promotion and appointment. Likewise, disruptive activities should count negatively. Similar criteria should apply to students.

Procedures for formulating policy

The would-be destroyers of academies have national organisations, and their attacks are carefully planned and co-ordinated. To be successful the defenders must also organise nationally and internationally to pool their intelligence and experience.

The law of the land applies everywhere. Likewise the internal codes of academies within a state should be in harmony. The destroyers know that higher education is indivisible. Their opponents must act similarly. In particular, the universities and polytechnics in Britain must combine to defend themselves. We therefore suggest that a national working party on higher education be established to draw up a Bill of Rights and Responsibilities, which should be adopted by all institutions of higher education. We suggest that the members of the working party should be mainly, but not entirely, academic, and should include representatives of the Committee of Vice-Chancellors of Universities and the Committee of Directors of Polytechnics. It should *not* include representatives of NUS, for general reasons deriving from the nature of academies, and for the particular reason that in Britain the NUS has an explicit policy of support for disruption.

We suggest also that there be established a Standing Committee, permanently available as an expert external source of advice and help for any institution subjected to disruption.

Protection of academic values

We contend that a commitment to dispassionate scholarship, balanced appraisal of issues, and honest criticism should be the concern of all members of the academy at all times. But such principles will not automatically prevail, especially if there are members of the academy who flout and exploit them. Hence the great importance of *communication*.

The institution cannot inculcate in the student a respect for dispassionate scholarship if, while ensuring strict standards in the seminar room, it ignores lies and distortions when presented in the campus newspaper, leaflets or speeches. Therefore regular, accurate and well-written information should be disseminated by the administrative and academic leadership to all members of the institution on all matters of importance. Every misinformation circulated, either deliberately or inadvertently, should be immediately and persistently corrected.

Neglect of this obvious rule has been disastrous at PNL. It is not enough to respond with leaflets in a crisis—although even this has not been done at PNL. If trouble is endemic it will be necessary to have a few persons continuously monitoring the information sources and sometimes actively intervening, with the backing of the institution, to prevent a crisis developing.

The institution should combine the practice of intransigence on fundamentals with a large degree of consultation on peripheral matters. This intransigence should be publicly proclaimed, i.e. the principles embodied in the Bill of Rights and Responsibilities should be continually drawn to people's attention.

If a crisis does develop the response should be one of 'aggressive tolerance', as described by Eric Ashby and Mary Anderson:[1]

> 'The cascade of propaganda which issues from duplicators during sit-ins may be—it usually is—composed of lies, innuendo, and the stale rhetoric of revolt. But it is a mistake to dismiss it as harmless trash. It puts the Establishment on the defensive and if the Establishment responds with nothing but silence or pompous resolutions, the thoughtful critical student may well begin to wonder whether the Establishment has a convincing defence to put up. The New Left declare that tolerance is repressive; their aim is to provoke an act of intolerance. Silence from the Establishment may create the impression that tolerance is weak. The proper response is not intolerance; it is (if we can give it a label) *aggressive* tolerance. Aggressive tolerance means that a university, threatened with some act of disruption, does not suppress it by force but by moral condemnation. This of course takes time. The prime tactic is to circulate continually, to staff and students, accurate and uncoloured facts, and also frank comment, preferably written by young members of staff known to have liberal views, about the relation between disruption and the articles of faith of a liberal university.'

They describe how in Chicago the University establishment issued frequent bulletins giving a 'Chronology of developments reporting . . . what the sitters-in were doing, what various committees were doing, what disciplinary steps were being taken'. These bulletins were supplemented by independent activities of staff and anti-disruption students.

Another aspect of communication is the *first impression* of the academy that the student receives. The Far Left in PNL are shrewd tacticians; this is clearly shown in their policy of all-out indoctrination

---

[1] *The Rise of the Student Estate in Britain*, Macmillan, 1970.

of students during the vital first weeks. From the
moment a student enters PNL he is subjected to a
barrage of one-sided information and false history;
and in the induction ceremonies the SU Executive are
prominent and aggressive, depicting the administration
and many of the senior academics as corrupt and
manipulative. We commend the practice of certain
institutions, such as the LSE, who do not permit this to
happen. Their induction programmes are organised by
academic staff alone.

A student whose first impression of an academy is
favourable will be the better learner because of it. The
main responsibility here lies with the academic staff,
for they are at the heart of all academic endeavour.

Libel

Sometimes stronger action is required than the mere
correction of false information. The Bill of Rights and
Responsibilities should prescribe criteria for libel and
rules for responding to it. The law of the land is not
sufficient. The possibility of the victim of libel having to
wait for two years and to face costs of some thousands
of pounds—even if he wins the case—makes the
courts useless to an academy in these matters. Cam-
paigns of libel or slander within an academy are
singularly damaging, since effective teaching depends
on trust and mutual respect.

Academic government

The disastrous performance of the PNL Academic
Board, with its large number of student members,
could have been predicted. It may serve as a warning of
what to expect if political criteria take precedence over
academic ones. It is likely that other academies will
experience pressures for 'reform' similar to those that
prevailed at PNL. We therefore suggest that national
guidelines on academic structure and government
should be formulated. The Privy Council has taken
some steps in this direction for the universities; the

proposed national working party on higher education could complete the task and advise the DES on the application of these guidelines to the polytechnics.

Another critical area covers the constitutions and financial activities of student unions. Clear national guidelines need to be formulated and applied covering such matters as electoral procedures for student union executive positions, representation on the NUS, and the sources and legitimate use of student union funds. These guidelines might include: limitations on the number of Sabbatical Officers and on the number of student seats on academic decision-making bodies— both could be related to the proportion of the student body voting in the relevant elections; national secret ballots for members of the NUS Executive; the wider use of referenda, both nationally and locally, for deciding student union policy; the funding of student unions by *voluntary subscription* rather than by a compulsory capitation fee which is usually paid by the student's Local Authority. Another area for national investigation could be the substitution of student loans for student grants.

*   *   *

We have described some ways of defending the academies against the determined parasites and predators who are now attacking them. In West Germany an additional device has been used: the formation of the Bund Freiheit der Wissenschaft (League for Free Scholarship). We recommend that a similar body be established in Britain, especially since an explicitly Marxist counterpart has already been formed here.[1]

The Bund Freiheit der Wissenschaft was set up in 1970 by university teachers, citizens and politicians of all constitutional parties (SPD, FDP and CDU). It aims 'to resist the left-wing radicals in the universities and

[1] *THES*, 9 May 1975. Centres for Marxist Education are being established in Manchester, Leeds, Sheffield and other cities.

to strike the radicals at their ideological foundations'. It has been very successful, which explains why its members are relentlessly attacked, provoked and abused. Among the factors in this success are the following:

- *(a)* Its members are both laymen and academics: 36 per cent professors, 14 per cent other university teachers, 7 per cent students, 45 per cent from outside the university.

- *(b)* It acts as a centre for the diffusion of information, to the press and elsewhere.

- *(c)* It has worked hard to arouse the 'mouse-grey' students, e.g. by running training courses for students in political argument and procedure.

- *(d)* It has insisted that the effectiveness of the reform of university laws should be evaluated by independent bodies such as parliamentary committees or external panels.

- *(e)* It has brought constitutional lawsuits against some of the university laws.

- *(f)* It has sponsored various fundamental reforms in higher education.

Prospects in Britain

Many will find it hard to believe that the left-wing totalitarians could ever be politically effective in Britain. Are they not too few in numbers, and are not the British too deeply liberal by temperament and tradition to support them?

We shall say briefly why we think that at this time the Far Left are well placed to have a large *destructive* effect.

The cultural revolution of the 1960s in Britain was an astonishingly forceful assault, obliterating in a few years much of the intellectual and spiritual accumulation of generations. For many people—especially the young—the foundations necessary for any coherent attitude to authority, or for building one's life on liberal values, were swept away.

Week after week the skilful satirists of *Private Eye* and BBC Television destroyed the faith of the young in those who occupied any official position or held to any enduring values. The satirists were ably assisted by the pop musicians—explicitly anti-liberal and indifferent to reason—who simply took for granted that anyone over the age of 25 was an idiot. These two groups were the main destroyers, but they were well supported by the playwrights and film-makers specialising in violence and pornography. A new mode of sensibility appeared: amoral, nihilistic and trendy.

This cultural revolution—apparently spontaneous —in which Britain was the pioneer for the Western world, was a key event. It made for a defenceless society, and it created the indispensable elements— the categories and shibboleths[1]—for the conspiratorial political revolution which is now being attempted.

The numbers of the New Left (IS, CP, IMG, Maoists, etc) need not be large, for they have developed remarkable skill at using the 'soft' liberals, a large class in Britain, sometimes cynically manipulating them as front men, at other times perverting liberal policies and values in the ways we have described. The Left know too how to exploit that major intellectual gap in modern liberal theory: the lack of an adequate analysis of authority. This use of the liberals has been essential in the attack on education. And there are many other influential liberals in Britain—opinion leaders in journalism, theology, economics, politics, for example —who by their failure to recognise these tactics are, however unwittingly, acting as valuable allies of the totalitarians.

It seems to us that Britain is in a more precarious position than West Germany. Its economy is less stable, its trade union structure is less rationalised and

---

[1] For example, to the mandarins of *Private Eye*, all members of the 'establishment' were musty, old-fashioned, arbitrary, absurd and corrupt.

more conflict-ridden, and the German people may well have learned some lessons in precautionary action from their two very bitter experiences in this century: hyper-inflation and the Hitler régime. Also, they have East Germany on their doorstep.

In Britain we are now confronting an extreme form of the classical liberal dilemma. How willing are we, in our academies and in society at large, to take the steps necessary to defend our institutions? And what will happen if we do not protect them?

A central purpose of this book is to make sure that people in Britain cannot give the excuse (used by many Germans about the events of the 1930s) that they did not know what was happening in their midst. But merely 'to observe this with indignation is pointless and ineffective because, as Bismarck said, "Indignation is not a category of political action".'[1]

The defenders of tolerance must now move to the attack.

---

[1] H. Schelsky, *op. cit.*, p. 626.

SELECT BIBLIOGRAPHY

Much of this book, particularly Chapters 2, 3 and 10, is extremely condensed due to lack of space. The following sources amplify many of our arguments and so may be useful to the interested reader.

*M. Oakeshott, 'Education: The engagement and its frustration', in R. J. Dearden, P. H. Hirst and R. S. Peters (eds.), *Education and the development of Reason*, Routledge and Kegan Paul, 1972.

*M. Reeves, 'The European University from Medieval Times, with special reference to Oxford and Cambridge', in W. R. Niblett (ed.), *Higher Education: Demand and Response*, Tavistock Publications, 1969.

*J. Searle, *The Campus War*, Pelican, 1972.

*R. Nisbet, *The Degradation of the Academic Dogma*, Heinemann, 1971.

K. Jaspers, *The Idea of the University*, Peter Owen, 1960.

*K. R. Minogue, *The Concept of a University*, Weidenfeld and Nicolson, 1973.

*E. Ashby, *Technology and the Academics*, Macmillan, 1966.

*G. C. Moodie and R. Eustace, *Power and Authority in British Universities*, Allen and Unwin, 1974.

*D. Martin, *Tracts against the Times*, Lutterworth Press, 1973.

*D. Martin, 'The Ugly Face of Participatory Democracy', *The Times Higher Education Supplement*, 5 April 1974.

*E. Ashby and M. Anderson, *The Rise of the Student Estate in Britain*, Macmillan, 1969.

C. Cox, B. Heraud, K. Jacka, J. Marks, R. Sullivan, 'Notes on the Polytechnic of North London', 1973 (copies available from the authors).

C. Cox and J. Marks, 'Student representation in Polytechnics', *Universities Quarterly*, Spring 1975.

*H. Schelsky, 'The Wider Setting of Disorder in the German Universities—The Strategy of "The Conquest of the System": The Long March Through the Institutions', *Minerva*, Vol. X, No. 4, October 1972, pp. 614-626.

G. N. Knauer, 'The Academic Consequences of Disorder in the German Universities', *Minerva*, Vol. XII, No. 4, October 1974, pp. 510-514.

W. Rüegg, 'The Intellectual Situation in German Higher Education', *Minerva*, Vol. XIII, No. 1, Spring 1975, pp. 103-120.

E. Shils, 'The Academic Ethos under Strain', *Minerva*, Vol. XIII, No. 1, Spring 1975, pp. 1-37.

*S. Wilson, 'Truth', Unit 10 of *Problems of Philosophy*, A303, Open University Press, 1973.

Carnegie Commission on Higher Education, *Dissent and Disruption*, McGraw Hill, 1971.

'Report of the Committee on Relations with Junior Members' (The Hart Report), Supplement No. 7 to the *Oxford University Gazette*, Vol. XCIX, May 1969.

'Report of the Sit-in in February 1972 and its Consequences' (The Devlin Report), *Cambridge University Reporter*, Special No. 12, Vol. CIII, 14 February 1973.

Lord Annan, *Report of the disturbances in the University of Essex*, University of Essex, 1974.

'Oration by the Senior Proctor for 1973-4' (esp. Appendix), *Oxford University Gazette*, 1 August 1974.

Counter-Bibliography

The following sources exemplify many of the viewpoints which we have criticised.

M. Teodori (ed.), *The New Left: A Documentary History*, Jonathan Cape, 1970.

A. Arblaster, *Academic Freedom*, Penguin, 1974.

A. Cockburn and R. Blackburn (eds.), *Student Power*, Penguin in association with *New Left Review*, 1969.

T. Pateman (ed.), *Counter Course: A Handbook for Course Criticism*, Penguin, 1972.

E. Robinson, *The New Polytechnics*, Penguin, 1969.

J. Pratt and T. Burgess, *Polytechnics: A Report*, Pitman, 1974.

D. Rubinstein and C. Stoneman, *Education for Democracy*, Penguin, 1970.

N. Berger, *Rights: A Handbook for People under Age*, Penguin, 1974.

INTRODUCING
. . . the Constitutional Book Club

In 1970 just as Mr Heath was setting up his ill-fated administration, Churchill Press launched the Constitutional Book Club. It was aimed particularly at teachers, students and other intellectuals who were prepared to question the 'progressive' consensus which had dominated politics, economics and morals ever since 1945.

Britain in Danger

In a declaration on the threats to our society, the sponsors singled out the increasing disruption by bullying minorities of industrial life and even of universities. At that time every attack on all forms of authority were publicised and even glamourised by the media, and especially by television. Under the heading *Time to Fight back* . . . we drew attention to the growing sickness in British society: the spread of violence, the undermining of moral values, the belittling of freedom, the decline in family and individual responsibility, the threat of inflation to our future and the erosion of such traditional values as hard work, honesty and the quest for honourable success in life.

The Challenge

The first title published by CBC was *Right Turn,* of which the *Financial Times* wrote:

> '. . . the dramatic emergence of what might be called the New Right—arguing tightly, logically and with great powers of persuasion—is eroding the grand consensus of socialism. The Constitutional Book Club is one of the manifestations . . . The challenge to the Left is one that they can no longer ignore . . .'

Membership

If you wish to join the CBC, you can either susbcribe £5 and receive copies of all eight titles listed overleaf —as long as stocks last—or £2·50 for the next three titles starting with *1985* . . .

CHURCHILL PRESS—CBC BOOKLIST

Editor Dr Rhodes Boyson

RIGHT TURN — 1970
A symposium on the need to end the 'progressive' consensus in British thinking and policy.

DOWN WITH THE POOR — 1971
An analysis of the failure of the 'welfare state' and a plan to end poverty.

TROUSERED APES — Duncan Williams (1971)
A study in the influence of literature on contemporary society.
BOOK OF THE YEAR choice of Malcolm Muggeridge, Peregrine Worsthorne, Ronald Butt, Shirley Williams.

GOODBYE TO NATIONALISATION — 1971
A symposium on the failure of the 'publicly' controlled industries and the need to return them to a competitive framework.

EDUCATION: THREATENED STANDARDS—1972
Essays on the present decline in educational achievement and suggestions for its improvement.

ONE MAN'S VIEW — Walter Salomon (1973)
An account of an individualist's crusade over twenty years on inflation, taxation, capitalism and liberty.

THE ACCOUNTABILITY OF SCHOOLS — 1973
An analysis of the present trends in education and suggestions to make schools more responsive to external standards and parental choice.

MUST HISTORY REPEAT ITSELF?
— Antony Fisher (1974)
A study of the lessons taught by the (repeated) failure and (occasional) success of Government Economic Policy through the ages.

Paperback editions available to CBC members at 75p a copy from 2 Lord North Street, London, SW1